OUR EARLIEST COLONIAL SETTLEMENTS

OUR
EARLIEST COLONIAL
SETTLEMENTS

*THEIR DIVERSITIES OF ORIGIN
AND LATER CHARACTERISTICS*

BY

CHARLES M. ANDREWS

GREAT SEAL BOOKS

A Division of Cornell University Press

ITHACA, NEW YORK

PREFACE

THE settlement of America by Englishmen in the seventeenth century was the first phase of that world-wide expansion of England which has continued for the past three centuries. The men who founded the colonies were Englishmen, the incentives that impelled them to migrate were English in their origin, and the forms of colonial life and government they set up were reproductions or modifications of institutions already established and conditions already prevailing in one way or another at home. The world of the colonies in the seventeenth century was an English world. The first duty, therefore, of him who would write of our colonial beginnings is to discover the place that each group of settlers occupied in this great colonizing adventure and to determine the exact character of the ideas and purposes of the founders in relation to the similar ideas and purposes that were influencing men at the same time in England. It is no part of his historical task to study the colonies from the vantage ground of later events or of the higher enlightenment of the present day in order to find out, as has sometimes been done with too vivid an imagination, the contribution that the men who settled the colonies have made to the principles and practices of the great Republic of today. Little that took place in America in the seventeenth century can be construed as American, in any proper sense of the word. To scrutinize that century for the purpose of extracting therefrom something analogous to modern notions of liberty and progress is to disturb the whole historical process and to run the risk of admitting prepossessions that have already done much to mislead the popular mind as to what the earliest period of English life on American soil really means. An unbiased approach to the colonies from the standpoint of their origin will do something to eliminate those patriotic and nationalistic obsessions that have often led to an interpretation of the American past in a manner rather ingenious and artificial than historical; while a comparative study of them in the light of the motives that gave them birth will help to clarify and define their remarkable individual peculiarities. The lectures here printed attempt to demonstrate the truth of some of these things.

C. M. A.

New Haven
September, 1933

CONTENTS

I

RALEIGH AND ROANOKE: THE PRELIMINARIES

COMMUNITIES have their biographies as well as individuals. In the organized life of groups of men, joined together under a common government for a common purpose, rather than in the lives of individuals or the literary productions of any age are we to find disclosed the hopes, aspirations, and progress of a people. As regards our colonial period in particular, biographical literature, whether contemporary or recent, gives us no clear picture of the life and activities of the colonists nor does it help us to understand the place that the colonies occupied in the general colonial scheme. Biography alone cannot reveal the underlying forces that were at work making for change and transformation, divergence and alignment, or do much more than represent the opinions and experiences of individual men. In their lives and writings individuals are far from always in accord with the spirit of an age, and even when in sympathy with it represent too often the whimsicalities, oddities, and prepossessions of the human soul. Furthermore, the literary output of our colonial period, unevenly distributed over the inhabited area, depicts sectional peculiarities rather than normal growth, and, taken by itself alone, presents but an imperfect view of the existing colonial scene.

The colonial settlements of the early seventeenth century were extraordinarily diverse in their origins and in the various conditions that accompanied their growth to maturity. These diversities in motive, circumstance, and organization were due in largest part to the one great fact that English colonization, in the beginning, was a matter of private enterprise. All settlements made by Englishmen in the Western World, whether on the Atlantic seaboard or on the islands of the Caribbean, were promoted by individuals or groups of individuals for purposes of their own. Our early beginnings were not the result of any common plan formulated by government or by men in authority for objects of state or for the acquirement of territory in the interest of national aggrandizement. Private initiative, with the assistance or connivance of those in office, formed the starting point of all our early settlements and plantations and, strengthened by state protection in the form of grants and charters, created that working compromise, so dear to the English heart, whereby citizens combined with one another to serve at once their own interests and those of the nation, at times and places of their own choosing. The outcome of this combination was manifold variety in an era of romantic beginnings, when each community exhibited characteristics that were peculiarly its own and expressed in its aims and purposes one phase or another of that struggle of the English nation towards a consciousness of existence, which had been an outstanding feature of the reigns of the Tudor sovereigns. In this movement, beyond anything that went before or came after, appears a richness of physical activity and spiritual discontent that is reflected in our early history. The struggle against Rome was a national struggle; the Elizabethan renaissance was a demonstration of national confidence and enthusiasm, of national independence and self-reliance; and the settlement of Englishmen in America was in like manner a national outpouring due to commercial ambition, territorial needs, and religious restlessness, all of which were motives at work stirring men to seek prosperity and betterment in other lands than their own.

Thus the fabric of American colonization is woven of many colors, representative of the diversified impulses and influences that were arousing the men of the sixteenth and seventeenth centuries to risk their lives and their fortunes in the world of the West. Some freighted their keels with the pure lust of excitement, seeking novel experiences in a region enwrapt with mystery and charged with that irresistible attraction which ever lures men onward towards the unknown. Some sought treasure and booty, aroused by the hope of riches from mines of gold and silver and seeing in the plundering of Spanish plate fleets a royal road to fortune and an opportunity for revenge on the Spanish colossus. Some, with an eye to a more legitimate profit, deemed the waters and coasts of the Western World a lucrative field for the investment of capital, and hoped for returns on their outlay that would double their fortunes and furnish an ample supply of those tropical commodities that were fast becoming a necessary part of an Englishman's daily life. Some, chiefly of the nobility, impoverished by the decay of their ancestral estates, sought to enlarge their landed areas and add to their revenues by acquiring new lands in the wilderness; while their tenants and farmers, in their efforts to earn a living for themselves and their children in their native land and seeing across the Atlantic boundless areas of unoccupied soil and no less boundless opportunities for the planting of homes and the rearing of families, joined the great migration for the one purpose of solving the most important of human problems—the problem of existence. And, lastly, a noteworthy group, with their eyes raised to Heaven but not eschewing the things of this world, came as religious pilgrims and dissenters, seeking an unmolested refuge and an opportunity to worship God in their own particular way.

These were the varied factors that created the diversities of settlement in the early seventeenth century. But equally essential to an understanding of our subject is an analysis of the activities of those men who were the precursors of the colonizing movement, for their efforts, though premature and unsuccessful, mark the beginning of that glorious and soul-stirring enterprise, dating from the days of Henry VII and Henry VIII, that resulted in establishing Englishmen in the lands beyond the seas.

To the era of forerunners, to the preparatory period in the history of English colonization, belongs Sir Walter Raleigh, the subject of this lecture. His activities are symptomatic of a time of discovery and exploration, of a dim, half-mythical period of bold adventure, filled with the deeds of individual heroes, daring and reckless men, which stands in such striking contrast with the later and more prosaic years of actual colonization. To the Englishmen at home the New World of Raleigh's day was still a realm largely of the imagination – the seas peopled with monsters, the lands dotted with cities of fancied magnificence and emboweled with mines of fabulous wealth. Men's dreams of the tropical world were as strange as were their superstitions, their belief in portents, their explanation of the mechanism of the human body, their interpretation of the solar system and other phenomena of nature. The age was one of discovery in more ways than one, but it was easier to explore the earth's surface than it was to penetrate the mysteries of the human anatomy or to unravel the laws governing the movements of sun and tide, earthquake and storm. Though Raleigh was able to sail overseas and to see much and to hear more of that which concerned the lands beyond the western horizon, he died three years before Harvey announced to his fellow men the epoch-making discovery of the circulation of the blood; and he suffered in his death from laws that were as crude in their application to social and political life as were the reasons men gave three centuries ago for the familiar phenomena of the physical universe.

The literature from which we gain our knowledge of the

exploits of this age of romantic endeavor is closely akin to that which tells of similar happenings in the childhood of other peoples than our own. Our epics and sagas are the tales and chronicles of voyages, told by the participants themselves or taken down at their dictation. These prose epics of the English and American peoples, some of which came from Portuguese, Spanish, and French sources, were collected, often translated, and finally published, first by Richard Eden in his *Decades of the Newe World or West India* in 1555, and later, towards the end of the century, by that lovable press agent of adventure, Richard Hakluyt of Oxford and Westminster. Hakluyt was one of the leaders of the movement. Though only a humble preacher, a gatherer of other men's tales, and a subscriber to voyaging enterprise, yet by means of his publicity he turned the thoughts of his countrymen towards the possibilities of the Western World. These voyages or "principal navigations," as he calls them, are veritable Odysseys of the sea, stories of wandering, suffering, brave deeds, and famous victories, calamities, successes, and sudden deaths; and, like all personal narratives unsupported by official or other authentic evidence, they are frequently open to suspicion as containing sometimes less and sometimes more than the facts, did we know them all, would warrant. For we must remember that very few official records appear to substantiate the chronicles of voyages—a few patents and letters of marque, a few entries of returns to the royal exchequer, an occasional reference to state interference, when, in excess of zeal against Spain, privateers in so-called "voyages of discovery" made trouble for the crown or its ministers and involved the government in some perplexities of policy. In the period of storm and stress, when the young English nation, rapidly growing to man's estate, was moved by the crusader's zeal for excitement and experience in a larger world, the state took neither lead nor responsibility, contenting itself with sanctioning or condoning private enterprise and sharing in some of the profits of marauding expeditions. Later, when the state entered the field and assumed the control of colonies that private energy had established, official records steadily increased and the personal narrative gave way to sources that bear an official stamp. The place of the saga was taken by the authoritative record, and the age of the Elizabethan adventure merged into the period of organized colonization and permanent settlement.

Of the many conspicuous individuals of this age of personal prowess none was more preëminent than Sir Walter Raleigh, none more loyally devoted to his sovereign and his country. But along with his finer qualities went a strange instinct for rapacity and a consummate skill in misleading others. He was at one time or another politician and courtier, soldier and sailor, historian and philosopher, often exhibiting adroitness, bravery, and a circumspection none too wise or well directed. He knew the ways of the court and played the gallant to his queen with the same ease that he trod the deck of a ship or deceived his mutinous sailors with promises of wealth from mines and galleons. He was daring even to recklessness and contumacy in his efforts to find in Venezuelan territory the gold of Manoa, and judicially calm as he gazed out over the world from his prison room in the Tower and essayed to write with dignity and dispassion the history of the human race. He could dissimulate with the cunning of a courtier when involved in the intrigues of the court and the commands of his royal mistress, yet he could face the block with an openness of soul from which all guile and untruth were purged, and utter that noblest of all his sayings, true epitaph of his better self, "what matter' how the head lie, so the heart be right?" There is no one connected with the early history of America who possessed and exercised such a variety of talents, for good and for evil, as did this courtier, philosopher, and seafarer of Elizabethan England.

Raleigh united in himself three types of adventurous activity, each of which had a place among the preliminaries of our colonial settlement. First of all, he promoted voyages of plunder and discovery, secret and lucrative privateering ventures that were concerned with a systematic robbery of England's enemies at sea; secondly, he himself sailed as registered sea captain into the heart of the Spanish Caribbean, leading expeditions in search of the gold of Guiana; and, lastly, his was one of the first English attempts to establish a colony on American soil. Thus he was capitalist, sea dog, and colonizer in one, covering in his ambitions more varieties of enterprise than any one else of his day. He never circumnavigated the globe as did Magellan, Drake, and Cavendish; he had no such tragically venturesome career as had his cousin, Sir Richard Grenville; and he never shared in the life of a colony as did William Penn and some of the Calverts. But he covered a wider range of overseas undertakings than any of these, and he may be allowed to bear that appellation, bestowed upon him by his friend the poet Spenser, of "Shepherd of the Ocean."

There is an interesting painting by Sir John Millais that represents the boy Walter sitting with a companion on the rocks at Budleigh Salterton in South Devonshire, gazing with rapt attention at a bronzed and hardy sailor, muscular and weather-worn, who as he spins his yarn points with enthusiasm towards the western horizon lying beyond the sweep of ocean visible in the background. No one seeing this painting can but feel the desire for adventure that filled the souls of the boys and men of Elizabethan England. Raleigh was born and bred in Devonshire, that land of bold mariners and early maritime activity; he was related to many Devonshire and Cornish families trained to the sea and familiar with its allures and its terrors; and he was thoroughly acquainted with the coming and going of men and ships from the near-by towns of Bristol, Plymouth, Dartmouth, Barnstaple, Bideford, and other centers of seafaring life and experience. He was at all times a sailor at heart and displayed through life a yearning and love for the sea that discloses itself both in his actions and in his writings. He was twenty-six years old when he reached the goal of his early ambition and, in conjunction with his half brother, Sir Humphrey Gilbert, took part in a voyage of discovery, as captain of his own vessel, during an unsuccessful expedition of six months. This first test of his powers bore witness to his love of action and quickness of resolve and to his coolness, daring, and confidence – efficient allies all of the spirit and hope that throughout his life burned within him.

Raleigh's training under the tutelage of his brother was received in the two expeditions of 1578 and 1583, which were set on foot primarily for discovery and settlement, but ultimately, as was inevitable at that time, for plunder and spoliation. That of 1578, in which Raleigh himself took part as captain of the *Falcon*, was originally designed for purposes of settlement, probably in Newfoundland, by way of the northern route familiar to all Devonshire fishermen. Gilbert, dreaming of a great landed estate for himself in America, had obtained from the crown, perhaps with Raleigh's help, a royal patent granting him wide territories with large jurisdictions and powers, wherever, under certain limitations, he might establish himself. Under that patent, he and Raleigh set forth from Dartmouth in September 1578. Dissensions arose, many of the company withdrew, those that set sail were driven off their course in a southerly direction towards the Azores and the West Indies, and the expedition failed. Gilbert afterward insisted that the failure was due to adverse winds and winter storms, "which was God's will not his," and declared that he had faithfully executed his promise to the queen to avoid plundering Spanish ships and towns. Had he not forbidden his company, he afterward wrote, "to do anything contrary to his word," and had he not "preferred his credit before his gain, he need not have returned as poor as he did." But, he added, he was not discouraged and would try again.

The next attempt was in 1583, when four of the six years allotted to his patent had expired and delay meant forfeiture and permanent failure. With Raleigh's aid and contributions furnished partly by friends, to whom he conceded grants of land, and partly by certain merchants, to whom he gave trade privileges in the new territory, he fitted out five ships with supplies and goods for barter, and in June set sail from Plymouth with two hundred and fifty men. Late in July he reached Newfoundland. Raleigh planned to accompany the expedition, but at the last moment, even, indeed, after the fleet had started on its course, he was recalled by his sovereign, at this time a woman of fifty and nineteen years his senior, who had no desire to risk the life of her handsome courtier in dangerous voyages on the sea. Thus Raleigh was prevented from taking part in the first expedition that sailed from England with the certain purpose of founding a colony in America.

Gilbert reached Newfoundland, displayed his authority, and took possession of the soil on which he intended to establish a great landed propriety. But the men whom he brought as prospective settlers were not of the stuff from which thrifty, law-abiding colonists are made, and the experiment came to a fatal end. Gilbert was drowned on a further voyage of discovery and the men whom he left in Newfoundland as tenants and servants on his estate, having no liking for the peaceful pursuits of agriculture and repelled by the bleakness of the Newfoundland coast, soon scattered and disappeared. Thus the first attempt at English colonization in America failed, partly because of the freebooting, unmanageable crowd that Gilbert tried to shape into a tractable body of settlers, and partly because of the fog-bound island – never a successful place of habitation during our colonial period – where he sought to locate his proprietary domain.

When Sir Humphrey Gilbert was lost at sea, one of the finest of Elizabethan heroes fell, a victim to his own waywardness and indiscretion. Buffeted by fortune, harassed by failure, dogged by fate and his own visionary and strong-willed nature, he stands as the first great English dreamer of a colonial empire in the West. Raleigh took his plan of colonization ready-made from Gilbert's hand; his patent for a proprietary domain was almost word for word the same as that which Gilbert had received; and the methods he employed were at first only an enlarged and improved edition of those that Gilbert had already tried. The latter was but forty-three years old when he was drowned, a man courageous and determined and in the prime of life. That he had planned to continue his efforts we know, and that he would have gained a greater measure of success had he lived is more than probable. We cannot say how far Raleigh helped him in forming his plans, but it is very likely that he had a considerable share in so doing and that what Gilbert proposed to accomplish was known to Raleigh in all its essential particulars. Raleigh had actually accompanied his brother on one expedition, and though forbidden to go in person on the second – the colonizing venture to Newfoundland – he had given it financial aid and had followed its fortunes and guarded its interests at home. Also, he was thoroughly alive to the necessity of continuing the task that his brother laid down at his death, and as partner in the enterprise and his brother's logical successor, he took upon himself the burden of carrying Gilbert's plans to a successful conclusion.

Gilbert was drowned in September 1583, and Raleigh must have received word of that tragic event before the end of the year. Three months later, in March 1584, a period none too long for the issue of a royal patent, he obtained from the chancery a charter of his own, conferring the same powers and privileges as those which Gilbert had received. A month later he dispatched his own first expedition, under the leadership of two experienced sea captains, with instructions to search for a suitable place in America where a colony might be established. Thus he lost no time in meeting the obligation that rested upon him of completing the work that his brother had begun.

But Raleigh was more than the mere executor of his brother's plans. He had ideas of his own and a worldly wisdom that his brother had not possessed. In many important particulars he improved on his brother's design and displayed a certain hard common sense and sagacity that Gilbert had lacked. In the first place, and in some respects most important of all, he would have nothing more to do with the northern route and with Newfoundland as the place for a colony. His reasons for this are not difficult to discover. He had been learning during these years a great deal about the Atlantic Ocean and the New World. He was an intimate of Richard Hakluyt, with whom he must have discussed these matters frequently, either in private conversation or in correspondence, for Hakluyt had issued his first work, *Divers Voyages touching the discovery of America*, in 1582, and in 1584 had published a *Particuler Discourse*, "at the request and direction of the right worshipful Sir Walter Rawley." In this way Raleigh had come into possession of many facts regarding the voyages of Spanish and French navigators and regarding the southern routes which they had followed. He had learned of El Dorado and Florida, of Spanish settlements and wealth, and of the richness and beauty of tropical life, and there can be no doubt that his mind was stirred not only by the desire to invade Spanish territory and plant the standard of his queen in the heart of the Spanish Main, but also by the hope of finding land not already possessed by a Christian prince or inhabited by a Christian people, as his patent required – one more propitious for colonization than were the inhospitable shores of Newfoundland. His plan was to seek the land of Florida, and, instead of a northern voyage, to follow the Spanish navigators in their southern course and approach the American coast by way of the West Indies.

In the second place, he enlarged the scope of the enterprise and placed it on a better financial footing. He must have realized that a colony, to be successful, should be composed of those who favored peaceful pursuits as well as acts of rapine and plunder, and that the boisterous spirits whom his brother had been unable to tame were sorry material for an orderly and well-governed settlement. Therefore, he called to his aid the best men that he could discover, and though inevitably he made mistakes in the selection of his associates, he attracted to his various undertakings the most remarkable group of men who up to this time had engaged in Western colonization. They formed a notable band – gentlemen corsairs, some of them, it is true, but all men of vigor and experience – while the commoners he enlisted seem to have been of the better sort.

The financing of the expeditions was well managed. Gilbert, though obtaining help from gentlemen and merchants, had been compelled to draw heavily on his own resources, spending, as he himself estimated, a thousand marks a year, until he was so reduced as to be obliged to sell the very clothes off his wife's back and at his death to leave her almost penniless. Raleigh, on the other hand, whose preferment at court began in 1581, was already enjoying large emoluments from licenses and monopolies, such as the queen was accustomed to grant to her favored courtiers, and was able to add to his own patrimony rich rewards and returns, not always honestly obtained, which rendered him financially independent and, unlike his brother, free to pursue his course without anxiety. He spent, he tells us, £40,000 on his various undertakings in behalf of colonization in America, and never received a penny of profit in return. Thus he stands at the head of that long line of ambitious and hopeful Englishmen of rank and wealth, who of their own initiative, unaided by the resources of court or government, attempted to establish settlements in the New World, without receiving interest on their investment or recovering any part of the capital that they had sunk in the work of founding a colonial empire. A few of these have reaped a posthumous reward in the names which perpetuate their memory, but many have gone down to oblivion, forgotten by the country which owes more to their sacrifices than most historians have been wont to assign to their credit.

With patent ready-made to his hand, with wide lands and wide privileges at his disposal, with a favorable route and a warmer climate already determined upon, with ampler resources, and with greater sagacity and knowledge of human nature, Raleigh in 1584 began that series of expeditions, partly for discovery and partly for colonization, that constitutes his chief claim to the gratitude and remembrance of the American people. On April 27 of that year, he dispatched "two barks well furnished with men and victuals," under the command of Philip Amadas and Arthur Barlowe, with Simon Fernando, a seafaring Portuguese of uncertain reputation, as pilot. Sailing southward to the Canaries and thence to the West Indies, they approached the American coast from the southeast, searching for a place suitable for a settlement. Somewhere about Cape Lookout, they must have smelled that "strong and sweet smell, as if they had been in the midst of some delicate garden abounding with all kinds of odiferous flowers," of which Barlowe wrote to Sir Walter. Coasting along the harborless sandbars northward, they finally entered one of the shallow and narrow inlets and took possession of the first land that greeted them, the island, as it proved, of Roanoke. After engaging in various tours of exploration and learning much about aboriginal life and habits, they departed in haste, having had but little time in which to make more than a cursory examination of the region, and returned to England, reaching there in September. They had been gone nine months and had traversed nearly ten thousand miles.

Their home-coming and the narrative which Barlowe furnished of their experiences, embellished probably by Raleigh in order to add to its alluring qualities, made something of a sensation at Whitehall, partly because of the novelty of the voyage and partly because it had been promoted by a courtier who was rapidly rising to the summit of the queen's favor. Elizabeth manifested her pleasure by naming the new country "Virginia," granting Raleigh the honor of knighthood, and further increasing his resources and influence. He was on the flood tide of prosperity and everything seemed to contribute to his success. He became a member of Parliament from Devonshire, was appointed warden of the stannaries or tin mines of Devon and Cornwall, and received large additions of territory from forfeited estates in England and Ireland. Thus favored and with the breath of the sea ever in his nostrils, he planned a second voyage across the waters. A colony in America promised to be the outcome of his efforts.

The new expedition represented in a remarkable degree the twofold motive that governed the men of Elizabethan England in all their undertakings. Mingled with the desire to attack Spain and to occupy territory which Spain claimed under the papal bull was the determination to extend as far south as possible England's hold on the Western lands. To effect these ends Raleigh selected as the leader of the new venture Sir Richard Grenville and peopled his ships with an unusually strong body of men – gentlemen and others – more than a hundred in number. Among them were Master Ralph Lane, second in command, Thomas Hariot, the historian of the expedition who wrote his famous book for the information of Raleigh, and John White, an English painter, whose designs, illustrating the manners and ways of the natives and the flora and fauna of the new land, were carried to Europe a year later and entrusted for engraving to the expert hands of the artist Theodore de Bry of Frankfort. All were dispatched from Plymouth, April 9, 1585. As might have been expected of the man whose desperate fight on the *Revenge,* six years later, is a famous incident in Elizabethan history, Grenville succeeded in both parts of his undertaking. He seized Spanish frigates laden with money and rich freights and likewise divers Spaniards whom he afterward ransomed for good round sums, and he deposited Master Ralph Lane with one hundred and seven gentlemen, commoners, and mariners on Roanoke Island, which Lane in his letter to Hakluyt declared to be "the goodliest and most pleasing territory of the world," where the people were "most courteous and very desirous to have clothes."

Though these settlers remained on the island for a year and explored the adjacent lands and waters for a circuit of many miles, north, west, and south, this first of Raleigh's colonizing efforts failed. Lane did not possess the tenacity and force of will that later enabled John Smith to hold together the Jamestown settlement. Despite his first favorable impressions, he was disquieted because he could find neither gold mines nor a passage to the South Sea, and he soon became convinced that the island and its neighborhood were unfit for permanent settlement because they possessed no satisfactory harbor. Hunger and troubles with the Indians weakened the spirit of these first colonists, and fearing lest help should not reach them from England, they seized the opportunity accidentally offered by the arrival of Drake off the coast to embark for home. Later Grenville returned with supplies and left fifteen men on the island in order to retain possession, but these eventually disappeared, having been killed by the Indians or drowned while attempting to leave the island. Thus ended a hopeful experiment – not a colony in the later sense of the word, but the most considerable settlement of Englishmen that had as yet taken place on the soil of America.

Though this first attempt at actual settlement had come to nothing, Raleigh was not to be turned from his purpose, and for the moment at least was determined to persevere. He bore among his many titles that of "Lord and Governor of Virginia," and it was his duty to make his title and patent good. Moreover, without colonists his great domain in America would be of no value, and if it remained of no value after so promising a beginning, the queen's displeasure, which he could not afford to incur, would certainly be vented upon him. Therefore, he gathered his resources together for a new enterprise, which in fact marks the first attempt to establish on American soil a colony possessing within itself the rudiments of an independent existence and so anticipates the later successful movement that established a new and living England within the frontier of the West.

In three important respects Raleigh's third venture was an advance upon the second. In the first place, it represented a different combination of colonists. Instead of men of the rough-and-ready, adventurous type, Raleigh sent men, women, and children, seemingly of the more domestic, peace-loving sort. Thus for the first time was assured to a settlement that continuity of family life without which even the best equipped of communities is bound to remain always an artificial, inorganic group of individuals. Of the one hundred and seventeen persons who sailed on the three ships provided for them, seventeen were women and nine children, some of them of tender age. It is a pity that we do not know more of the circumstances under which this company was brought together or how it was that seventeen women – two with children yet unborn – the first to cross the Atlantic from England, were induced to make this perilous voyage. Probably John White, the leader whom Raleigh selected, was the responsible agent in the matter.

In the second place, Raleigh organized a definite form of government by appointing the same John White deputy governor under himself as chief, with twelve others – all from the class of gentlemen – as assistants and advisers in council. There is ample reason, also, to believe that he drew up a body of instructions, stating in detail the conditions under which government was to be carried on. Unfortunately, these instructions have not been preserved, but as they concerned the government of the "City of Raleigh in Virginia" it is likely that they were designed to reproduce, in a measure, the borough organization of England, a type essentially different from the military system which Gilbert had attempted to apply in Newfoundland and which Lane had enforced in his first settlement at Roanoke. Though there is nothing to show that Raleigh had in mind anything that may be likened to a popular management of affairs, he did provide for something that promised to be permanent and that might in time take on a popular form.

Lastly, Raleigh charged White to find for the colony a better place than Roanoke had shown itself to be. Acting probably on the information that Lane had furnished and on the advice of Hakluyt, who in December 1586 had written him a letter to that effect, Raleigh instructed White to follow the coast northward to Chesapeake Bay and there to choose a satisfactory site for the city and fort that he wished to become the nucleus of his new propriety.

Had Raleigh's plan been as carefully carried out as they were wisely framed, we might have a different tale to tell of the issue of the enterprise. Perhaps if he himself could have led the colony in person across the ocean, sharing its hardships, directing its activities, and exercising his prerogatives as governor in chief, he would have won imperishable renown as the founder of the first English colony in the New World. But this was not to be. He could not leave England, where he was entangled in the meshes of the queen's favor, burdened with the responsibilities of the wardenship of the stannaries and the vice admiralty judgeship of the west, involved in land schemes in Ireland, and bound to his post as member of Parliament. He was dabbling in too many things, was concerned in too many ventures, and was trying in too many ways to combine gallantry with business to give adequate personal attention to his interests across the sea. In consequence, his colony went its own way to its own undoing, lost, never to be heard of again.

Nor were those whom Raleigh selected to aid him in his various colonial plans gifted with the qualities of wise and constructive leadership. Grenville had shown himself to be hot-headed, impatient, and rash. Lane, though energetic and resourceful and not lacking in valor, became convinced of the unsuitableness of the place. Unable to find either gold or passageways to the South Seas, and fearful of privation and suffering, he had become discouraged early in the experiment. Finally White, deficient in executive ability and firmness of will, allowed himself to be overruled at critical junctures, and displayed bad judgment in returning to England a month after his arrival, leaving the colony without a head. Contrary to Raleigh's express command, the landing was made at Roanoke, which was no fit place for a colony or even for continuous habitation, while the storms of Hatteras were a menace to sailing vessels and gave to the coast an evil reputation among sailors. According to White's tale, this initial blunder was due to Simon Fernando, the pilot, who by refusing to land the colonists at any other place than Roanoke prevented them from going to the Chesapeake; but whether Simon was the real villain of the play, a great villain or a small villain or a villain at all, we do not certainly know. The charge is White's and White had some need to exculpate himself.

A more convincing cause of failure was the lack of supplies from England. The landing was made in July 1587; in August, White embarked, and not for four years, till August 1591, did he see again the spot where he had left his company. No colony at this early period could have held out against such neglect. Had the little group of men at Jamestown received no supplies whatever between 1607 and 1611 it would have required more than the efforts of John Smith or any one else to have kept them alive. Starvation was the archenemy of the early colonists. Those of Popham in 1607 and of Robert Gorges in 1623 were driven back to England by fear of starvation, and Jamestown, Plymouth, and Bermuda each had its period of starvation.

But why were supplies not forthcoming? It may be that the captains and sailors were afraid of the coast and could not be persuaded to go there, even on so humane an errand. But I am not sure that this statement is convincing. The ships that reached Roanoke earlier—those of Amadas and Barlowe, Lane, Drake, Grenville, and White—seem to have had no serious difficulty in making their way, and there is nothing to show that those which were sent to the rescue, five times between 1588 and 1602, failed in their mission because of storms and dangers from shipwreck. Grenville's voyage of 1588 was drawn off on a prize hunt for Spanish ships; that of White in 1591 was also delayed by a search for plunder; while the three that followed took the southern route and "performed nothing," some following "their own profit elsewhere" and others returning "with frivolous allegations." That of 1602 under Samuel Mace, "a very sufficient mariner and honest, sober man, who had been twice before in Virginia," was deterred, it is true, by fear of shipwreck, but only because his ship had already suffered damage. Even Raleigh himself, when in 1595 he went in person on his first expedition to Guiana to seek a new realm for his queen and to pour into her lap the golden fruit of that "large and bewtiful" country and so to regain her favor, seems never to have dreamed of turning aside to discover the whereabouts of his lost settlers. It is difficult to believe that the seamen of Elizabeth's day were deterred from a work of rescue by fear or timidity or were possessed of a spirit so at variance with the traditions of the British race. It was not the fear of shipwreck that sacrificed the colonists of Roanoke; it was the terrible allurement of wealth and the no less terrible hatred of the Spaniards, "that cruel and insolent nation," that "nation of ravenous straungers which more greedily thirst after English blood than after the lives of anie other people of Europe." Englishmen were defending what they deemed was the justice of their cause "against the ambicious and bloudy pretences of the Spaniards," "who," as Raleigh himself wrote, "seeking to devour all nations are themselves devoured."

The simple truth is that the chivalrous attempts which Gilbert and Raleigh made to plant colonies in the New World were inopportune and premature. They represented an idea for the application of which the world was not yet ready. England before the age of Elizabeth had been too poor to indulge in colonization and too weak to risk an encounter with Spain. Victory over the hated enemy had first to be won before colonization could be successfully undertaken. The passion that stirred men's souls was not the desire for peaceful conquest; it was a warlike zeal born of the indignation that Englishmen felt because of the "bloudy and injurious designs of the Spaniards . . . purposed and practiced against all Christian princes, over whom they seek unlawful and ungodly rule and empery." During the years from 1580 to 1596 this passion was at its height, and until its intensity was relieved by the breaking of the Spanish power, successful colonization was impossible. During these years every expedition that set forth from English shores took on a semipiratical form, seeking booty, capturing ships, or otherwise wreaking a crusader's vengeance on the despoilers of the world's peace. The very ships that were sent to rescue the lost colonists felt it a part of their stern but patriotic duty to "spoil the Egyptians" even while pursuing their errand of mercy. Making war upon Spain, not the planting of colonies beyond the ocean, was the motive determining the direction of Elizabethan activities. For seventy years after the Armada, even while successful colonization was well under way, this warlike quest, as a well-defined part of the Parliamentarian and Puritan policy, was relentlessly pursued, not by kings but by adventurous captains, merchants, and trading companies, until the menace of Spanish supremacy was removed by the peace of the Pyrenees in 1659. By that time England had obtained a permanent hold upon some of the richest parts of the declining Spanish empire.

Even if the spirit of the time had been favorable to colonization, it is doubtful if Raleigh would ever have appreciated or understood the difficulties of the problem that confronted him or envisaged the part colonies were to play in England's imperial career. One function of a colony, he believed, was to serve as a weapon wherewith to humble the pretensions of Spain and to press the claims of England to a part of the world that Spain was appropriating to herself, for Elizabeth denied the right of the Spaniards to the whole of America by virtue of the donation of the bishop of Rome. It is true that later he beheld, as in a vision, the planting of a new England in the West, when he wrote to Robert Cecil, just before his ruin, "I shall yet live to see it an Inglishe nation"; but it is hard to reconcile his words with his own efforts, wasted in the attempts of 1595 and 1617 to find in Guiana the mines of Manoa, or with his persistent pursuit of the golden quarry of Spain, which finally brought him to his execution in 1618. It may be that an adequate explanation lies not only in his great enmity for Spain, but also in the tragedy of his own career when he took a gambler's chance, hoping for wealth wherewith to bribe the wisest fool in Christendom, and thereby to unlock the gates of the Tower and so to save himself from the block. But the fact still remains that he was never sufficiently tenacious of purpose to pursue any scheme, colonizing or other, to the end that success demanded. His activity took a myriad of forms, in which a craving for fame and publicity and an itch for gain were the ruling influences. He was never imbued with the loftiness of design or the singleness of resolve that characterized the efforts of Calvert or Penn, or even of Shaftesbury; and as later events were to show, the transplanting and successful rooting of a colony in America demanded something more than the equipping of ships and the transporting of colonists. It required the wealth and organized coöperation of the capitalistic classes of England, the religious zeal of the Pilgrims and Puritans, and the continuous and persistent efforts of the Calverts, the Penns, and the Carolina proprietors.

When compared with the settlements of Virginia, New England, Maryland, the Carolinas, and Pennsylvania, Raleigh's experiments in colonization seem but half-hearted endeavors, in which skill and material were lacking.

I have spoken of the wealth and organized coöperation of the capitalistic classes of England. The subject is important, for without the resources of accumulated wealth neither courage, persistence, nor religious zeal would have been of much avail. To colonize America required not merely the support of those who were lords of the soil, wage earners of the towns, and tenants on the manorial estates, but also the active participation of the rich bourgeoisie, a class hardly existent at the beginning of the Tudor period but now rapidly rising into political and commercial importance, ready to invest their reserves of capital in any form of profit-bearing enterprise. Hitherto, they had spent their wealth in acquiring landed properties in England, outfitting ships for piratical ventures against the Spaniards, and organizing companies for the prosecution of trade and commerce—companies that had operated chiefly in old and settled countries, along the North Sea, the Baltic, and the Mediterranean, where trade, not land or colonies, was the object. Up to this time they had not been impressed with the importance of colonization in the New World as offering opportunities for profitable investment.

Both Gilbert and Raleigh recognized the growing influence of this moneyed class and endeavored to enlist its aid in furthering their undertakings. In a measure Gilbert was successful, though he obtained his chief support from gentlemen of his own rank. Raleigh depended on his own resources until 1589, two years after the failure of his last expedition, when, apparently realizing that his own career as a colonizer was at an end, he made over some of the privileges of his patent to nineteen merchants and others of London, organized as a voluntary association for the purpose of furnishing merchandise, munitions, victuals, and other commodities in exchange for rights of trade and other perquisites. Hoping to gain their coöperation in carrying on what he had already accomplished, he gave them £100, admitted them "free trade and traffic for all manner of merchandise or commodities whatever" in his seignory of Virginia, and promised to obtain for them, if he could, legal incorporation as a trading company under royal letters patent. There is no evidence to show that the merchants were ever incorporated or attempted to act in any way under the agreement, but to this arrangement we can trace the beginning of the movement which was to lead to the settlement of Virginia, seventeen years later.

The time for a trading company to take the lead in colonizing America had not yet come, but it is significant that some of those or the sons of those to whom Gilbert and Raleigh had turned as sharers in their enterprises became members of the Virginia Company, chartered in 1606, under the auspices of which Jamestown was settled. Knowledge of America and interest in its development grew rapidly in those intervening years, and we are probably justified in considering Raleigh's association of merchants as the forerunner, if not the nucleus, of the greater company to come. Raleigh saw the value of middle-class support and anticipated that combination of capital, commerce, and the colonies which was to become the mainspring of England's colonial and commercial greatness. But he saw it as in a glass darkly, as a hope rather than a fulfillment, for not until the next century was capital ready to face the colonial problem. Raleigh lived to see the dawn of the new day, but by that time his own active interest in colonization had passed away forever. Though he foresaw, as with the eye of a prophet, the importance of the New World as a land not of gold but of living men, though he appreciated the value of permanent settlements inhabited by people cultivating the soil and producing raw materials for the benefit of the mother country, and though he forecast one phase of England's future when he wrote, "He that rules the sea, rules the commerce of the world and to him that rules the commerce of the world belongs the treasure of the world and indeed the world itself," he was never able to conjure up a vision of the political destinies of America or of the democracy and popular self-government that were to be. He was himself an aristocrat, a member of the small landed class of the feudal type, hedged in by all the sympathies and limitations of his order. The nation that he pictured in America was modeled on the English nation that he knew, a nation in which social, industrial, and tenurial relations were shot through and through with the ideas and practices of class and caste. He was no utopian, as were Sir Thomas More, Roger Williams, and Thomas Hooker; no religious or political dissenter as was the Puritan; no political reformer, even, as was the Parliamentarian under the Stuarts. His England was a manorial and monarchical England and his America would have been a manorial and monarchical America likewise. He never conceived of conditions in political and social life that were other than those of which he had learned from the past, or with which he was familiar as one who had lived in England during the reign of Elizabeth.

Raleigh was more than an outstanding figure in an age of conspicuous men. He was more than an Elizabethan courtier possessed of versatility, rapacity, ambition, and love of action. He was the first Englishman to demonstrate the practicability of transporting English men and women overseas to find new homes on a new soil. His colony of husbands and wives, mothers and nursing children, in which births took place, baptisms were performed, letters written and tokens sent, where peaceful industry prevailed and order reigned, represents a new departure in English history. His was a type of colonizing community hitherto unknown to Englishmen and destined to be ignored for many years to come, but it stands out like a good omen in the warlike and lawless annals of the time. The experiment was premature and never received the test of continuance, but it was planned in the spirit of wisdom and its failure was the failure of circumstance. Just how much it contributed to the later and successful enterprise we may not conjecture; for though some of its lessons were forgotten by those who renewed the experiment in different parts of the colonial world in the next century, it is difficult to believe that it was without effect as a preliminary effort. The city of Raleigh was in very truth the forerunner of the city of James, and had the settlement at Roanoke survived the blows of an unkindly fortune, it might have achieved fame as the oldest of the many plantations in the Western World, from which has sprung the United States of America.

II

VIRGINIA: A NORMAL ENGLISH COLONY, THE FIRST GREAT EXPERIMENT IN ENGLISH COLONIZATION

O F all the colonies settled on the mainland of America in the early seventeenth century, Virginia was the only one that, strictly speaking, represented England's own commercial and economic expansion. In its long unbroken history of continuous growth and enlargement it presents all the characteristics of a normal colony. No one of the other settlements can compare with it in the length of its membership in the British family, in the uniform and consistently forward flow of its political and economic life, and in the completeness with which it seemed to conform to the English expectation of what a colony should be. In order to play its part in the fashioning of the great republic, it had to rid itself of little that was either religious or proprietary, and throughout its career it exhibited few traces of those religious and feudal influences that characterized New England and Maryland. It followed the mother country very closely in its land law and law of descent, in its ecclesiastical organization, in the procedure and practice of its assembly, and even in the form of its legislative chamber, which reproduced very closely St. Stephen's Chapel where the House of Commons sat in England. It was the most highly prized of all the crown's possessions on the Atlantic seaboard and was better known than any of the others to the officials at home. Virginia holds a unique and important position among the colonies, for her story is that of a homogeneous people, little affected by foreign racial influences, gradually unfolding, in a process of normal colonial development, from a primitive insecure settlement of a few hundred souls into a powerful community of more than half a million people. In the origin and growth of the settlement on the James we can find exemplified, better than anywhere else, the difficulties that accompanied the great experiment of English colonization in America.

England's situation in 1607, when Virginia was founded, was the culmination of more than a century of gradual transformation from a position of third-rate importance among the powers of Europe to one of leadership in the markets of the world. Owing partly to the growth of a commercial spirit and to a quickening interest in the seagoing activities of the day, and partly to the example of other maritime peoples, notably of Portugal and Spain, Englishmen were gradually awakening to a new ambition and a new ardor. Though slow to respond to the importance of overseas advantages, they were beginning in Elizabeth's reign to participate in the opportunities which the old and new worlds were offering to all, and to overcome the obstacles of serious import that for many years had obstructed the path of adventure beyond their own shores. Political and religious controversies – products of the Reformation in England – had absorbed their time, energy, and resources. Economic and social changes, due to the decay of feudalism and the consequent displacement of population, had raised new domestic issues incident to a period of industrial transition and a shifting of the center of political gravity from the local communities to the national government. Wealth in the form of mobile capital had hardly as yet accumulated in quantities abundant enough to meet more than local and immediate needs, and geographical knowledge and familiarity with the ocean routes were still insufficient to encourage distant voyages or to arouse interest in dangerous expeditions to unknown lands. Englishmen of that day found large parts of the eastern market already controlled by foreigners; they saw journeys westward blocked by the barriers of a forbidding continent; and they knew that exploration to the southward was menaced by the dominant control of the Spanish crown.

But rapidly the situation was bringing its own remedy. The last days of the Venetian mastery of the English carrying trade were drawing to their close. From 1509 to 1518 no Venetian fleet had visited England and trade had declined so steadily that in 1532 the Venetian Flanders galley had sailed from Southampton for the last time. Individual Venetian merchants continued to deal with England for some years to come, but their enterprise came to an end with the wrecking of a Venetian vessel off the Isle of Wight in 1587. The *Jesus of Lübeck*, purchased in 1564, was the last foreign-built ship to enter the service of Queen Elizabeth. The special privileges of the Hanseatic League were canceled by the queen in 1578 and through the activities of a small group of London merchants – the monopolistic Merchant Adventurers, fast rising into prominence – the Hansards were expelled in 1587, and the steelyard, their station on the banks of the Thames, was handed over to the City of London the next year. Though the leaguers attempted to recover a part of their privileges later, the loss of their station was a witness to the fact that at last the English had obtained control of their own commerce. The Merchant Staplers, oldest of England's trading organizations, the members of which were engaged in exporting raw wool and going to and fro between England and the Continent, were passing away. Calais, their chief staple town across the Channel, was seized by the French in 1557, and Antwerp, also an entrepôt for English wool, was sacked in 1567 and again in 1585. Thus England was gradually severing the ties that bound her as a commercial dependency on the foreigner and as a satellite of the Continental powers, and for the first time was ready to go alone.

Local and private traders had already begun to organize themselves under that form of consolidated enterprise known as the "company," the beginnings of which, though modeled on the pattern of the medieval guild, represent a new idea in corporate organization. In the century from 1555 to 1698, during which the "company" became the prevailing type of industrial economy, these bodies controlled every variety of progressive business activity – domestic and foreign – and there was scarcely any financial adventure or any part of the eastern civilized world in which they were not to be found. They carried England's trade into remote corners of the globe; they aided private undertakings, such as the search for the northwest passage; and they were to be responsible for the first successful beginning of English colonization in America.

The period after 1604, when peace was made with Spain, which lasted for some twenty years, was a time of marked improvement financially in England. This was particularly true of the outports of the West Country, which had suffered a serious decline with the rise of London during the later years of Elizabeth's reign. It was a period of recuperation from the evil effects of the "boom in privateering" which had accompanied the long-drawn-out struggle with Spain, for it once more opened the ports of Europe to legitimate trade and made it possible for English commerce to enter upon a new era of prosperity. Capital, no longer diverted from its authorized channels to war expenditure, once more became available for peaceful investment and money came out of hoarding or increased in amount in the natural course of business. It was no incidental circumstance that led to the planting of Jamestown in 1607, for the period from 1604 to 1620 was a time of peace, prosperity, and confidence in the future, and it was during this period that the first steps were taken towards the permanent colonization of the New World. Also the period was one of mental and social unrest, when much that was medieval was running concurrently with the beginning of modern things; when political and intellectual conditions were in a state of flux; when feudal tenures were adapting themselves to a new agriculture; when medieval methods of education seemed challenged by a new spirit of inquiry; when the old empiricism was giving way before the new experimental methods, and the medieval concept of law and government was being shaken to its foundations by the force of a new individualism. Then it was that Englishmen began to turn to the West as well as the East, interested not only in the expansion of trade but in the expansion of England also. Though clinging to the past, they were beginning to dream of a future in which a new world was to have a place. In the field of colonization the men of England were on the eve of their first contact with almost unknown lands and a great adventure was about to begin.

It is not surprising that at this juncture English capitalists, already familiar with voyages of western exploration and some of them directly interested in the Raleigh enterprise of only seventeen years before, should have sensed the opportunity of investing money in a colonizing expedition overseas. It is not surprising that they should have turned to a corporate company as likely to be more successful than had been the private adventurer of the Raleigh type and that they should have believed that a joint stock would be stronger and more effective for the purpose than the resources of a single man, however energetic and distinguished he might be. It is not surprising, either, that when their plan was put into execution and the famous charter of 1606 was obtained, it should represent the coöperation of the two rival commercial centers of the day, London and the outports of Plymouth and Bristol, and should take the form of a dual corporate group – the Virginia companies of London and Plymouth. Nor need we wonder that King James, who cared more for his own prestige and authority than he did for economic questions of any kind, should have retained in his own hands the general control through a royal council in England and should have limited the powers of the two companies to matters of equipment and administration only. The whole undertaking was an experiment, and the English authorities were merely following the familiar practice of separating the two functions of policy and administration, retaining one in the king's hand and leaving the other to the company; that is, to the active business agent.

There are two parts to the Virginia story: that which concerns the company in England and that which concerns the colony in America. The latter in the past has been greatly overstressed by American writers with a liking for the biographical and picturesque aspects of history, and its career has been worked out in detail as fully as the meager records for the period will allow. Unlike three of the other colonies which we are considering — Rhode Island, Connecticut, and Maryland — the leading interest of the subject will center not so much in the colony as in England, where lay the company which founded and nurtured this, the first English colony in America. In every other case the government and ultimate authority eventually lay in America and the connections with England were slight and relatively unimportant; but for the greater part of our period, the colony of Virginia was almost entirely dependent on the company at home for its very existence. It was itself but a tiny offshoot in a distant land, a small group, at first of men but later of women also, which looked to England for its additions to population, its stock of cattle, its instruments of labor, its methods of distributing land, and its manner of government. For many years it did almost nothing on its own initiative. As time went on it acquired a certain amount of economic independence through the discovery of tobacco as a profitable staple for export, and it was granted a certain amount of political independence when it was allowed the privilege of a popular assembly; but for seventeen years it drew its life from the Virginia Company, as a child draws its life from the mother that gave it birth. We shall deal with events in the colony only as far as they are affected by events in England and by the rise and fall of the Virginia Company.

The story of that company has been shamefully neglected by our historians, who have focused their attention almost entirely on what was happening within the colony, and, when dealt with at all, has been treated with so much prejudice and injustice as to distort the whole account. Only recently, and for the first time adequately, has the story of the decline and fall of the Virginia Company been told with thoroughness, fairness, and excellent judgment. It is the story of the effort of a joint-stock company to found and build up a colony, to bring about success where hitherto there had been only failure, and to decide the question whether that particular kind of corporate organization, which had been so effective in the field of commerce and trade, was fitted to enter the field of colonization also. In that field the problems to be solved were bound to be totally different from any that had been faced before and, therefore, difficult to anticipate; and, to meet them, preparation and experience were prerequisites to success. The experiment had not gone far before changes were found to be imperative, and two new charters had to be obtained before the company reached that degree of strength and efficiency which was essential for the proper performing of its functions.

It is strange that those in command should have learned nothing from the Raleigh experiences, except in the one particular of avoiding Roanoke and settling on the Chesapeake. They sent as their first installment of colonists a set of rough hardy men of any class or quality, drawn together in large part by the love of adventure and the prospect of gold and plunder, and in lesser part by the need of employment, thrown out as some of them were by the cessation of war in 1604. These men were similar in kind to those that had gone before in nearly all the colonizing ventures thus far made – in Newfoundland, Maine, and on the Guiana coast. Their selection shows that colonization, associated with the idea of profit and plunder, was still in its infancy and had not advanced to the later stages of trade and the agricultural life. The promoters had not yet realized that a colony to be permanent should root itself in the soil, that it should be self-perpetuating and self-sustaining, increasing its population by additions from within as well as by accretions from without, and raising its own food instead of waiting for supplies from home. It took Englishmen a long time to learn that a settlement to be successful had to rest upon a more certain foundation than the desire for wealth obtained from booty or the cult of the metals, or even from trade and traffic with the Indians. Because the men who first occupied Jamestown were not of the kind to plough and cultivate the soil, the entire absence of domestic life rendered inevitable a continued dependence on outside supplies, both of food and men. Thus it was that in those earlier years the colonists were brought face to face with starvation and with the complete wreck of the whole undertaking. The historic importance of John Smith lies, not in his relations with Pocahontas – an insignificant incident, whether mythical or otherwise – but in the fact that during his two years in the colony he compelled the drones to bear their share of the burden, and threatened that if they did not work he would drive them forth to starve in the wilderness.

During the first three years the experiment approached dangerously near to unqualified failure, and it began to look as if the fate of Sagadahoc in Maine, the first enterprise of the Plymouth Company, would be the fate of Virginia also. The colony, badly mismanaged, was in danger of starving. Endless quarrels, bickerings, and factional disputes kept the place in a constant state of disturbance, until the company in England realized, after long debate, that the government both at home and in the colony would have to be changed radically. For the first purpose it obtained a new charter in 1609, which got rid of the royal council and placed both control and management in its own hands. It then became in outward form a joint-stock company of the usual type, and the control, formerly in the hands of a royal council, was transferred to the company itself, which was given full power and authority to correct, pardon, and rule those inhabiting the colony according to such ordinances as it might provide. For the first time the entire direction of affairs was vested in the company – not in the whole body of its members, but only in the governor, who was called the treasurer, and his council. Under this arrangement the company planned a new system of government for the colony, and made a wide appeal for funds, issuing broadsides and prospectuses, and even calling on the clergy to preach sermons in its behalf. The appeal was not very successful, and it began to look as if those with money to invest were not at all sanguine as to the future of the colony and were unwilling to send good money after bad. It began to look, also, as if the fault lay with the organization at home instead of with conditions in Virginia, and after three more years of experimentation the leaders of the enterprise began anew the scrutiny of the charter. Four defects were found. In the first place, the English discovery of Bermuda in 1609 and the probable value of the islands to the company made desirable an extension of boundaries, for Bermuda had not been mentioned in the charter of that year. Secondly, dissatisfaction was rife within the company because of the unequal distribution of powers, as the members – the generality or stockholders – met very infrequently and were without influence in the councils of the company. Thirdly, experience showed that even the treasurer and his advisers had insufficient authority to apprehend and punish troublesome offenders, such as defaulting employees, mutinous seamen, and abusive colonists. And, lastly, the unsatisfactory state of the finances demanded that some other source of maintenance be found than by voluntary subscriptions, which thus far had proved discouragingly insufficient. All of these defects were remedied by the third charter, that of 1612, which marks the final form in which the organization was cast and embodies the ultimate powers which the company possessed. Bermuda was now added to its territory; control was vested in the whole body of the members, meeting in four great courts a year, at which all might be present, thus giving to the system a character that was strongly "democratical," as contemporaries called it; the powers were greatly enlarged, as the company was vested with the right to apprehend, examine, commit, or bind over for their good behavior any notorious offenders. Finally, the company was authorized to erect one or more lotteries each year for the raising of funds, an authorization that the king reinforced by a special proclamation. Thus after six years of haphazard effort the company seemed to be prepared to cope with the difficult problems before it and to bring to a higher level of perfection the management of its colony in America. How well it succeeded later events are to show.

In the meantime, what of the colony in America? After the issue of the charter of 1609 the company, with full powers in its hands for the first time, determined to change the form of government there and to substitute for the council of many members with a president at its head a single and absolute governor with an authority so extensive as to make him almost a dictator for life. It was a dangerous experiment, which was given a test for nearly eight years, and the men selected as governors of the colony – Gates, Dale, and Argall – have been anathema to the old-time historians of Virginia. Later writers have understood the situation better and have treated these men with more circumspection. They have realized that the harshness of the rule has been enormously exaggerated and that the laws which were laid down were never in force as a whole, the worst of them having been designed not for actual use but only for the terrifying of evildoers. Something had to be done to rid the place of lawlessness and to improve its reputation at home as a well-managed and peaceful colony. Furthermore, the age was one of physical violence, and the infliction of pain by whipping and mutilation was a usual form of punishment. It is much to be doubted if Gates or Dale would have been condemned by unbiased men of their own day who were used to the brutal and revolting practices in vogue in England at the time. Dale's strict régime was greatly modified before he left in 1616, and the laws themselves were gradually withdrawn during the ensuing two and a half years. Nevertheless, the policy, itself an experiment in colonial administration, was a mistake. That severe laws and arbitrary methods were needed to restrain the lawlessness of those few but troublesome men who had come from the jails and slums of London and other English cities and from the ranks of the unemployed can hardly be denied, but that such laws and methods aided in any way to increase the prosperity of the settlers or to make the people more contented can well be questioned. The settlement had now been in existence for nearly twelve years and even yet the company at home had not learned how best to govern a colony three thousand miles away.

The enlargements of 1612 vastly strengthened the company and increased its influence and prestige. This had been brought about by extending its territory, adding to its judicial authority, arousing anew the interest of its members, and giving it as a source of revenue the lottery, which was afterward spoken of as "the real and substantial food by which Virginia had been nourished." Furthermore, the broadening of the activities of the members by admitting them to the councils of the company, and the establishment of a common fund, designed for the promotion of the welfare of the colony, placed the company in all respects on a regular joint-stock basis and enabled it, in a manner unknown before, to expand and enlarge its enterprises. In consequence, during these years the condition of the colony gradually improved, and, although the quality of the settlers was still far from satisfactory, there were sent over fewer soldiers of fortune, men of action, and gallants who were trying to escape evil destinies. Women joined the colony, lands were distributed for private cultivation, and the discovery of tobacco and better methods of curing it prepared the way for a surplus staple product that was eventually to become the mainstay of the colony. The appearance of families—wives, children, and servants—shows that the company at last was beginning to understand what a colony ought to be.

But the reorganization of 1612 brought evils in its train —evils inherent in the joint-stock system. The most important of these was the great increase in the number of stockholders, due to the sale and transfer of stock and to a certain amount of stockjobbing—infrequent, perhaps, because of uncertainty as to profits—which brought into the membership many whose interest was mainly financial. Others were admitted, without payment, for meritorious services, for skill in artisan work, and for aiding in the dispatch and transfer of colonists. The numbers subscribing were the greater because of the fact that no oath of allegiance to the company was required as was the case with other joint-stock organizations. As all who were admitted could be present at the general courts and take part in the proceedings, it inevitably resulted that votes were manipulated, parties and blocs formed, and the election of officials and the adoption of policies became matters of heated and prolonged controversy. From this time forward some of the worst features of "democratical" control began to appear in the management of affairs.

The first serious outcome of this condition of things appeared in 1619 when a shift of leadership was effected. Up to this time the treasurer and leading spirit in the enterprise had been Sir Thomas Smith, perhaps the most conspicuous merchant and company promoter of his day. He and his great rival, Sir Edwin Sandys, had both been members of the council under the charter of 1609 and had continued to work together amicably enough after 1612. Both had concurred in the situation in Virginia under Gates and Dale, and there is nothing to show, as the records for those years have been lost or perhaps were intentionally destroyed, that their ideas regarding the centering of authority and the distribution of powers differed sufficiently to affect the operations of the company. But circumstances were soon to arise that brought into the open a series of personal rivalries and factional disputes, in which Smith, Sandys, Sir Robert Rich, later the Earl of Warwick, and others were so deeply involved as to bring about the disruption of the company and its eventual dissolution. Smith and Warwick came into conflict over certain appointments in a subsidiary and little-sister corporation, the Bermuda Company, and the rift was widened because of Warwick's freebooting activities that brought him into trouble with the East India Company of which Smith was governor. Other causes increased the antagonism. Sandys and his followers charged Smith with mismanagement of the accounts and, anxious to obtain an opportunity to perform certain experiments of their own in Virginia, were making every effort to secure control of the company. Sandys and Warwick drew together and, aided in the management of the voting by the use of the secret ballot, which with many other practices had been borrowed from the procedure of the East India Company, ousted Smith from the leadership and elected Sandys in his place. Henceforth, Smith ceased to take any important part in the company's affairs. How far he deserves the charges that the Sandys party brought against him it is difficult to say. The settlement of Virginia was only one and a minor one of his manifold activities, and he was better fitted by experience to deal with matters of trade than with matters of colonization. He treated the settlement of Virginia as a business enterprise, to be handled somewhat as he handled affairs in Muscovy and the East, and he probably failed to grasp some of the social and economic needs that had to be met if the colony were to prosper. Furthermore, he was so overburdened with responsibilities that he probably was accustomed to leave details, both of administration and of accounts, as in the matter of the books of the company, to subordinates; consequently, the results might well have been unsatisfactory to members of the company. He died in 1625, perhaps the greatest single figure not only in the mercantile world of the early seventeenth century in England, but in the world of the colonies also. He it was who promoted more than any other single man the founding of Virginia and nursed the colony along, under most discouraging circumstances, to a successful rooting in the soil of the New World. Important as John Smith was and great as has been his fame, he was not nearly so important in the history of Virginia's settlement as was that other member of the Smith family, Sir Thomas, whose name has been largely lost to sight among the more colorful characters that are associated in the popular mind with Virginia's earlier years.

The change in the leadership of the company and the beginning of factional quarreling which accompanied it has in the minds of many writers tended to overshadow somewhat the more important aspects of the company's management of its colony during these eventful years. From about 1617 to 1622 was a period of feverish activity among its members for the purpose of putting the colony on a sound social and economic foundation and of reshaping its whole political and legal structure. The period is divisible into two parts, one representing the projects undertaken while Smith was still treasurer, planned by all the leaders acting together – a remarkable body of reforms that were wisely conceived and energetically carried out; and the other, characterized by the sanguine and overwrought efforts of the Sandys and Ferrar party, ambitiously contrived and lavishly executed, which overburdened the company's resources to its eventual embarrassment and disorder. Let us examine these periods briefly.

In 1616 in the colony the joint management of land and stock, begun in 1609 to continue for seven years, came to an end, and the opportunity arrived for establishing private ownership of the soil and of making it possible for the colonists themselves to obtain a profit from the work of their own hands. The company apportioned unoccupied lands for private use and public purposes – so much for individuals, so much for the ministry, so much for the college which it hoped to found, and so much for the company itself. For the peopling of the public lands it sent over large numbers, not only of planters but also of servants and apprentices, and dispatched shiploads of women as wives for the settlers, in order to widen the scope of family life and make the men more settled and contented. It sent over children – boys and girls – drawn from the alleys and byways of the cities of London and elsewhere, and a few felons from the jails of Middlesex. Many of the newcomers became tenants and the servants of tenants, some on private lands, some on the company's own lands, and all were to labor for the profit of the undertakers and the prosperity of the colony. The leaders in England, resenting the tendency towards the cultivation of tobacco as the sole staple of the colony, made every effort to force the colonists to produce a wider variety, such as grain, hemp, grapes, licorice, and silk grass, and to engage in certain industrial pursuits, such as the production of naval stores, potash, glass, and the setting up of sawmills and ironworks. For this purpose they dispatched not only English artisans but also skilled workmen from other countries—Poles, Germans, Swedes, and Italians. Though these industrial ventures came eventually to untimely ends because the lure of tobacco was too strong to be overcome and capital, skill, and cheap labor were all wanting, nevertheless, at the beginning they gave promise of success and were persisted in for many years.

In some ways most interesting of all were the encouragements given to groups of persons, either of the company or from outside, to aid in the populating of the soil and the advancement of its agricultural life. From 1616 to 1623 many groups of associates received patents of land under certain very liberal conditions for the purpose of promoting the occupation of the soil and of adding to its productivity. "Divers lords, knights, gentlemen and citizens," as the record reads, "grieved to see this great action fall to nothing . . . offered to take the matter anew in hand and at their private charges, joining themselves into societies, to set up divers particular plantations." This practice of inviting the coöperation of private persons to aid the company at their own expense was not peculiar to the Virginia Company. It was a characteristic practice of other colonizing companies, and even the Massachusetts Bay Company in New England employed it to a small extent. These particular plantations had somewhat the character of private colonies, with powers of self-government under their own chosen officials, subject only to the higher authority of the government of the colony in political and legal matters. A number of these plantations were actually set up in Virginia, and continued to survive for many years, destined eventually to be absorbed into the common system and to lose their identity. They stand as one of the many forms of experimentation employed at the time as to how best to increase population and strengthen the economic life of an English colony in the New World.

But the most important reform and reorganization of this period was the drafting of the great charter of grants and liberties, prepared sometime before November 1618, at a time when Sir Thomas Smith was still treasurer and Alderman Robert Johnson was his deputy, and when Sandys and Warwick were still on friendly terms. This, the "greate Charter," as it was contemporaneously called, was the company's sufficient reply to the complaints that had been accumulating of Argall's way of governing Virginia, for it put an end to the rule inaugurated by Gates and Dale and introduced a system of popular coöperation and government in colonial affairs that was undoubtedly copied from the practice of the company itself in its quarterly gatherings of the generality in England. The charter outlined at great length the revised method of making land grants, gave rules for the location of new plantations, and said something about quitrents and taxes – regarding the last of which we would gladly know more. It provided for proper relations with the Indians and contained instructions for an efficient management of trade and the best method of handling the staples of the colony. It probably included also a statement of the plans of the company for the setting up of particular plantations and promised that the colony should be henceforth governed by the common law and magistracy of England instead of by the more or less arbitrary methods and laws of the former governors. It was a document that dealt chiefly with trade, land, and law, but it had a political bearing also, for it instructed the new governor, Yeardley, to call, soon after his arrival in the colony, a general assembly of the planters. The object of such a concession was to gain the good will and participation of the colonists in matters that were economic rather than political, and to secure their approval of the company's plans rather than to concern themselves with the passing of laws as such. What the company wanted was peace, prosperity, and profit, and it was willing to allow the colonists in Virginia, as it was, at almost the same time, to allow the colonists in Bermuda — for we must remember that the same men ran the two companies — the privileges of Englishmen as regards their law, government, and general economic order. This assembly, which met in 1619, is an important landmark in the constitutional aspects of colonial experimentation; but it must be kept in mind that, like the Bermuda assembly, it was brought into existence by the company as a whole and not by any one man or set of men. In fact, the Bermuda assembly has in some ways a stronger claim to our remembrance, because, barring a few years' suspension under one of its governors, Sir John Heydon, it can boast of an unbroken history from the beginning to the present day. That, as we shall see, was not true of the Virginia assembly.

All these things were accomplished before Sandys rose to the headship of the company. By that time the colony, though still suffering from sickness and death and hardly as yet on its feet as a successful agricultural community, was already beyond the experimental stage and promised well for the future. Sandys and others of his party took hold of the situation with enthusiasm and a vigorous but undisciplined imagination. Their minds ranged over the whole group of the company's interests and saw in a number of important particulars opportunities for advancing the welfare both of company and colony. They proposed, first of all, to apply for a new charter for the company, in which the name "governor" should be substituted for "treasurer," and "Virginia" for "Southern Virginia," which should confer still larger privileges and immunities such as would attract a more stable body of subscribers and, when confirmed by act of Parliament, should place the company in a better position "to strengthen the plantation in general by engaging the whole state in the interest and support of the action." This plan was proposed in 1620, at about the same time that the Plymouth Company was securing its new charter, but it was never carried to completion. Just why, I do not know certainly, unless the reason be a lack of funds, for the passage of a charter at that time cost a good deal of money.

In the second place, they wished to set on foot a more regular and systematic way of meeting the needs of the colony, by sending over a continuous series of ships, with men, provisions, utensils, and money; by making arrangements in the colony for churches, inns, guest houses or hospitals, a free school, and a college; by enlarging the list of colonial staples; and by sending more skilled artisans, artificers, and gardeners wherewith to widen the economic base upon which rested the prosperity of the colony. This part of the plan was carried out, during the years from 1621 to 1623, with great animation and stoutness of heart, so that in 1622, when the massacre by the Indians took place, there were 1,240 people in the colony and the outlook for the ironworks, salt works, the breeding of silkworms and the making of silk, the producing of flax and hemp, the manufacture of glass beads for the trade with the Indians, and the multiplying of the stock of English and Irish cattle seemed reasonably bright. The colony in that year was possessed of all the essentials of a permanent settlement— family and agricultural life, men, women, and children, artisans, tenants, hired laborers, indentured servants, and a few Negroes. Its numbers were increasing from within and without; its supply of oxen, cows, swine, and goats was growing rapidly; forty-two sail of ships was reported in 1623 as plying back and forth between England and the colony; and in the main the people were peaceful and contented.

But the financial condition of the company was very precarious and becoming worse. At this juncture, with the treasury practically empty, subscribers refusing to pay up, and others unwilling to subscribe, a catastrophe occurred. The king withdrew from the company the privilege of holding the lottery. This method of raising money, started in 1612, and successful from the company's point of view, had stirred up a good deal of opposition in other quarters, for the people of the towns in which the agents were at work complained of the demoralizing effects of their methods upon trade and industry, caused by the popular excitement which the lottery aroused. In March 1621, at the request of the House of Commons, the Privy Council ordered "that the further execution of the lotteries bee suspended" and this was done by proclamation four days later, as necessary "for the public good." That this suppression was a royal device wherewith to injure the company, as used to be believed, is rendered impossible by the fact that the king and council acted on the recommendation of the House of Commons.

The raising of money by other means now became an imperative necessity. Sandys and the Ferrars were not good business men; they were unable to command in the business world the confidence that Sir Thomas Smith inspired, nor had they at their command the methods or the financial shrewdness that had characterized their predecessors in office. Unable to increase the joint stock of the company in the regular way, they tried a variety of supplemental measures. They continued the issue of grants for particular plantations. They adopted on a scale larger than ever before the device of the subordinate and voluntary joint stock by creating associations from among their own members for all sorts of purposes – the making of glass and beads, the providing of apparel of which the colony stood greatly in need, the sending of women as wives for the colonists, the prosecuting of trade with the Indians, and the dispatching of shipwrights and other principal workmen for making ships, boats, and other vessels. In 1620 they revived the magazine, which was not only to continue as the company's store in the colony, but was also to provide cows, mares, goats, asses from France, and maids and apprentices. But all these were mere palliatives to help out a difficult financial situation. A more permanent source of revenue had to be found, and this was discovered, as the leaders fondly hoped, in the profit from tobacco. To this end they endeavored, during the year 1622, to enter into a special tobacco contract with the king.

There is no opportunity here to discuss the involved and tortuous negotiations that accompanied the effort made by the company to effect a satisfactory arrangement with the crown for the handling of the surplus tobacco that the colony could furnish and that England needed. Suffice it to say that, despairing of their attempt to persuade the Virginians to raise other staples or to engage in industry, Sandys and his party accepted, unwillingly and only for the time being, this outstanding staple, tobacco, as a very ready help in time of trouble. They saw in it the only commodity that might serve them in their financial distress, and they sought to perfect an arrangement with the crown whereby the company might assume the monopoly of tobacco importation under conditions that would be advantageous to all concerned. On November 27, 1622, at an extraordinary court held for Virginia, this contract was approved by a majority of both the Virginia and the Bermuda companies and the bargain was ratified by the Privy Council the February following.

The debate on the tobacco contract disclosed the existence of a powerful opposition to the Sandys party in the general court. The members of this opposition did not want the contract. It is probable that some of the Sandys followers did not want it either, but, rather than break with the king, accepted it as "a bitter pill," even though they feared it might be "prejudiciall unto them in matter of profitt." So strong was the opposition that many members left the meeting of November 27 before the vote was taken, claiming that all were overawed by the chairman, the Earl of Southampton, who had succeeded Sandys in 1620. The antagonism thus aroused was greatly intensified when the method of managing the monopoly was presented for consideration. An elaborate list of officers with large salaries was offered the meeting for acceptance, and the incumbents named were chiefly taken from the party of Sandys, Southampton, and the Ferrars. Two chief objections to this scheme were raised in the meeting: the salaries were too large for the financial condition of the company; and the officers named disclosed (as the opposition said) an attempt on the part of Sandys and his followers not only to line their own pockets but also to get a firmer hold on both company and plantation. This opposition, led by Sir Nathaniel Rich, cousin of the Earl of Warwick, Alderman Johnson, and others, appealed for relief to the lord treasurer, Lionel Cranfield. He, aroused by the bickering and factional quarrelings that now accompanied all the debates in the general court, decided that the whole matter should be inquired into, each party to present its own case. The inquiry took place, first before the lord treasurer and then before the Privy Council, and in the end the latter, April 28, 1623, ordered that the contract be dissolved as tending "to the utter overthrow and subversion of the whole plantation." The tobacco contract was dead.

The situation of the company in 1623 was desperate. The splendid activities of the early years were giving way before the acrimonious debates of the years that followed. This relaxation of effort was in part due, no doubt, to the great Indian massacre of 1622, which checked further attempts at expansion in the colony and brought to an end its industrial enterprises. But it was due in greater part to the financial bankruptcy of the company, which, having lost the privilege of the lottery and the benefits, whatever they were, of the tobacco contract, with all sorts of petitions and complaints coming in, seemed helpless to meet the situation. It had kept no registry of people going to the plantation, had provided no way by which families and friends could get in touch with those who had gone overseas, and was seemingly impotent in such matters as keeping a check on passengers' goods and enforcing covenants between masters and servants. It had set up no probate system in the colonies, so that the fate of those who died in Virginia – and there were scores of such, many of whom had relatives and property in England – remained unknown, except as returning colonists brought the news. Such neglect must have caused not only personal sorrow but also much business confusion. When to these manifestations of inefficiency we add the many demands that were made upon the company for recompense and wages and the suits of law that were threatened, we can understand the widespread belief that the Sandys party had wasted the substance of the company and that the so-called "democratical" way of conducting affairs, leading to bad management, political manipulation, and a resort to all sorts of devices for the purpose of maintaining party control, was proving a lamentable failure.

With the growing financial embarrassment of the company and the failure of the plans for the betterment of the colony, the factional disputes and the savage personal dislikes which had been steadily increasing since 1622 took on increasingly bitter forms. The meetings were attended by disorderly and unworthy persons, the proceedings were accompanied by violence and turmoil, and outside the place of assembly two members of the opposing parties engaged in a fight and two others almost engaged in a duel. Within, hard words were bandied back and forth, lies passed, and threats made. By the end of 1623 the prestige of the company was so seriously overcast that its usefulness as a colonizing agency was greatly impaired. The colony, still bearing the scars of the massacre and in a pitiable condition from bad and insufficient food, was stumbling along without guidance and without support. No money could be raised at home, the earlier ambitious undertakings were brought to an end, the stream of settlers and supplies from England either dwindled to very slender proportions or ceased altogether. The members of the company were so entangled in a labyrinth of charges and countercharges that there appeared to be no way out of the maze. Extrication from the predicament had become, as John Chamberlain wrote to Sir Dudley Carleton, "a thornie business," and to many a man of the day there must have seemed no other solution than to get rid of the company altogether.

The royal government now stepped in, and in reply to a petition from Alderman Johnson sent in April 1623, the king ordered the Privy Council to investigate the situation. With the utmost fairness was this investigation conducted. Both sides were given every opportunity to present their respective cases at hearings held before the king, the lord treasurer, and the Privy Council. The Sandys party carried the matter into Parliament, although the issue was one which belonged only to the executive branch of the government and with which the legislative branch had nothing to do. Sandys took this course because he thought that the chances of success would be the greater if the dispute could be made a political rather than an administrative issue and if a decision could be reached on political grounds rather than on a fair study of the merits of the case. But the king took the matter out of the hands of Parliament, partly because it did not belong there and partly because it was likely to breed "much faction and distraction," and he handed it over to a commission that was instructed to make a searching inquiry. At the same time he ordered the Privy Council to manage the colony until it was once more on its feet. This the Privy Council did, compelling the company to resume its support of the colony, which it was shamefully neglecting.

The simple truth is that the Virginia Company had reached a point where it was unable to meet its obligations and, to use a modern phrase, was obliged to go into the hands of a receiver, there to remain until the king, acting under the advice of the commission he had appointed and of the crown lawyers whom he wished to consult, could decide upon its eventual fate. The advice, offered after careful consideration, was that the company might retain its colony, provided it would accept a new charter, which was to be modeled after the old charter of 1606. This the company refused to do, the surrender being voted down by all but nine members on October 20, 1623, in a court from which Warwick, Rich, and other opposition leaders were conspicuously absent. On hearing of this refusal, the attorney-general immediately made application for a writ of quo warranto, and after a trial, which was twice postponed, the decision of the court of King's Bench was rendered, May 24, 1624, against the company. The Virginia Company had ceased to exist.

The fall of the company was due to its failure as a colonizing agency. The effort of older writers to show that political influences were at work – that there was a court party against a patriot party; that Warwick, as an ally or tool of a tyrannous king, was in a plot to defeat the designs of the liberals, Sandys and his friends, whose aims were in the interest of progress and popular government – all this has no justification whatever. For such an interpretation no contemporary evidence exists and its iteration at the hands of American historians is merely another instance of the survival of the Whig tradition that has done so much to misrepresent and falsify American colonial history. The fall of the company was due to mismanagement, to the internal dissensions that arose among its members, and to the attempt to carry out, on an insufficient and precarious capital, an overambitious and unwise program of colonization. As an instrument for the control of a distant plantation, in a new and untried country, where self-support was difficult and sickness and death were a daily occurrence, a joint-stock company organized on a "democratical" plan proved too loose-jointed and hydra-headed to be effective.

With the disappearance of the company, the colony was left, more or less alone, to work out its own salvation. Happily, by 1624 it was fairly well established on Virginia soil. It contained a population of twelve hundred people, which in four years rose to three thousand, occupying the tidewater region from Chesapeake Bay to the Falls of the James River. This area was very flat and low, ascending gradually not more than two hundred feet for the entire distance of fifty miles. The effect of tobacco planting and cattle ranging was to scatter the population and prevent it from gathering at any point in towns or compact communities. Jamestown was the seat of government and the port of customs entry, though tobacco might be shipped from any of the plantations along the river. The houses there and elsewhere were for a long time very modest structures, because money was scarce and labor expensive, but there, during portions of the year, government was carried on, business was done, fairs were held, and life was fairly gay and festive. Taken as a whole, the colony was made up largely of small planters and not of wealthy landowners. All the earlier industrial enterprises had failed, and except for a small amount of shipbuilding and the necessary construction of houses and other buildings all artisan activities had ceased. The efforts to make glass, iron, potash, and wine had all come to an end, and Virginia entered on its career as an agricultural colony, with its future dependent on a single staple — tobacco.

After May 4, 1624, Virginia was a royal colony, the first to come into the hands of the crown, and the colonists were confronted with the momentous question as to what the king intended to do with them. The experiment was not yet complete, for with the fall of the Virginia Company there was no certainty that the king would continue the same policy as that which the company had inaugurated, particularly in the matter of a representative gathering of the inhabitants for the purpose of coöperating in government. Bermuda offered no precedent, for it was and continued to be for fifty years in the hands of a company and not of the crown. It may be said at once that no attempt was ever made by England to interfere with the system of land tenure and law which was already established in the colony. The common law of England remained the law of Virginia and the land system underwent only such modifications as came about naturally in the course of its development — the private plantations, the public lands, and the college lands gradually being absorbed into the common system.

What the planters were most afraid of was the restoration of the arbitrary government that had existed before 1619. In petitions that were sent in, some of them even before the company was dissolved, they asked for five things: first, that the local council be allowed to act as a restraint upon any governor that might be sent over; secondly, that the general assembly be retained, "than which nothing can more conduce to our satisfaction and the publick utility"; thirdly, that the governor lay no taxes or impositions upon the colony, their lands, or commodities, otherwise than by the authority of the general assembly, to be levied and employed as the said assembly should appoint; fourthly, that no tobacco contracts be entered into that would be to the disadvantage of the planters; and lastly, that the company be not restored.

Now, in regard to these matters, a very interesting situation presents itself. The Virginia plantation had been in existence as a going concern for seventeen years – with many ups and downs of fortune, owing partly to mismanagement on the part of the company in England and partly to the exigencies of life in the colony. It had weathered most of its troubles and had passed the most dangerous crises of its career. Despite the terrible Indian massacre of 1622, which had cost the colony four hundred seasoned men and women and reduced its population to about eight hundred, and despite the almost hopeless outlook for the ironworks, the salt works, and the other industrial enterprises, in the presence of the ineradicable desire to raise tobacco, Virginia in 1624 was largely a self-supporting colony, capable in the main of looking after itself. Therefore, we find that without much regard to what was taking place in England the colony was going ahead on its own account and under its own power, little troubled by the authorities at home; that is, by the king and his advisers, in whose hands legally lay the future control of the colony. In fact, of the five points mentioned already, two were left for the colony to settle for itself, the other three being the only ones ever seriously considered in England. These three were the question of the revival of the company, the calling of a general assembly (which had ceased to meet after the fall of the company), and the making of arrangements regarding the importation of tobacco of such a nature as would be advantageous to the colony. This last point was undoubtedly the most important that troubled the colonists during these critical years, for upon it rested the economic prosperity of Virginia, and in those days economic prosperity was more to be desired than political privileges.

It is not necessary here to enter upon the complicated story of the various commissions, committees, and delegations that attempted to decide what should be done about Virginia from 1625, when the death of James I put an end to one set of appointments and required the naming of another, until the establishment of the Dorset commission in 1631, which was the last of the series. The issue at stake was a serious one, for the king could do what he liked with his own, and the future of all royal colonies lay in the balance. Would he or would he not revive the company? Would he or would he not attempt to enter again into some form of tobacco contract, which might prove disadvantageous to Virginia and weigh heavily upon the planters there? Would he or would he not continue the government by governor and council, which had come into being with the fall of the company, or would he concede the right of an assembly to meet as it had done for five years?

The first point, the revival of the company, was actually under advisement for sixteen years. In 1631 the first petition for revival was refused "as altogether inconvenient for his Majesty's service both here and there." But the members of the old company persisted, only to be turned down again in 1633. Again and for the last time the matter was brought up in 1640, and though the demand was made an issue in the Long Parliament, where if anywhere the so-called liberal party might have got redress, it was dismissed without action, and Charles I on appeal refused to take it into consideration because he and his advisers deemed it contrary to the interests of the kingdom. Thus ended the long struggle for the restoration of the Virginia Company, which failed because of the general impression the factional quarreling had made, not only upon those in authority but upon those in general who were interested in trade and colonization, and because of the manifest preference of the colony for an immediate dependence on the crown.

The second point, the matter of the tobacco contract, after debate at home and consultation with the colony, was satisfactorily settled and need not be discussed further here. But the third point, that of the general assembly, cannot be so summarily dismissed. It was not a matter easily or quickly to be disposed of, and we cannot but conclude that the authorities in England shirked a decision in the case and left the whole matter to be determined by the colonists themselves. From 1625 to 1629 occasional gatherings of a sort, made up of representatives from the boroughs, were called together for the purpose of dealing with certain special issues, chiefly economic, but not for lawmaking or the levying of taxes. They cannot be called legislative bodies in the sense that they were successors to the assemblies from 1619 to 1624. But from 1630 to 1638 general assemblies did meet, though we know very little about the way they were brought together, that passed laws and performed many of the usual functions of a parliamentary body, and it has been commonly supposed that they did so legally. As far as we know, however, the king during these years made no sign and issued no authorization to his governor to call such bodies together. If that is the case, then, not one of these assemblies was a legal gathering. Any assembly in a royal colony during our colonial period that met without a fresh writ of summons from the crown, issued by the governor properly instructed to do so, was illegally and unconstitutionally convened. The people of Virginia knew this, for, half a dozen times during this decade from 1630 to 1638, they sent petitions to England begging the king to confirm their privileges, while continuing to meet in assembly, confident that the crown would approve their action and validate their laws. But it was not until the instructions to Wyatt were drafted in 1639 and those to Berkeley in 1641 that at last the English authorities made up their minds, and, in proper and legal language, authorized the governor to call the representatives of the people together annually for the making of acts and laws for the government of the plantation. It is a curious situation. The colonists had been doing this very thing, without interference from the crown, for nearly ten years, never inquiring whether or not their laws were contrary to those of England and rarely if ever sending them over for the inspection of the king in council. The people of Virginia forced the king's hand, and it is to their everlasting credit that they did so, for from this time on, with but few exceptions, and those only temporary, the rule was established that a royal colony in America was to be governed not by a governor alone, not by a governor and council acting in their executive capacity, but by a governor, council, and assembly, king and people sharing in the lawmaking and tax-levying powers of the government.

This first successful experiment in English colonization lasted for more than thirty years before it reached its first maturity as a normal colony of the royal type. Virginia by 1640 had become the model after which, in the years that followed from that day to this, was to be shaped England's system of royal control of crown colonies on the political and administrative sides. In this momentous decision the Virginia planters had no small part, for they had shown, by example, that the people of a colony were to be entrusted safely with a coöperative share in its government. This decision was strictly political and constitutional, for it had nothing to do with the economic and commercial life of the colony. A final settlement in that particular was not to be made until many years later, when England was brought face to face with the even more important question as to what the commercial relations were to be between the mother country and its colonies. But the earlier decision was of great significance. Though self-government in those days even in Virginia was hardly democratic, and though popular interest in lawmaking was never very keen in colonial times, nevertheless the very presence of a popular assembly in a royal British colony in America was a factor of vast consequence in the development of American political ideas.

III

MASSACHUSETTS:
A PURITAN COMMONWEALTH, THE
DESIGN OF WHICH WAS RELIGION

WHILE in many parts of the American world – in New-foundland, Bermuda, the West Indies, the regions of the Orinoco and the Amazon, and even in parts of New England itself – normal processes of colonization similar to those of Virginia were at work, some successfully and others unsuccessfully, a new factor, of an entirely different character, was making itself felt. Though religion as a motive for colonization was generally present in all the enterprises, it served, as a rule, no higher end than the crusader's desire to convert the heathen. In no settlement outside New England was religion the sole directing force, though elsewhere at one time or another in the course of a century were to be found Roman Catholics, Quakers, Huguenots, Moravians, Mennonites, Mystics, and Pietists, who had escaped from lands where they were unable to live their lives as they wished. Men and women of England, France, and Central Europe migrated to America because they were prevented from gathering in meetings or churches of their own religious persuasion at home, from ordering their social and family connections according to what they believed was the purpose of God in his relations with men, or from controlling the opinions and practices of others in matters of ecclesiastical polity, religious creed, and social conduct. But no one of these religious groups founded a colony the sole design of which was a new order of religious organization and discipline. Each became but a part of a larger whole, content with such measure of religious freedom and opportunity as it was able to secure, and, except perhaps for the Quakers in Pennsylvania and Rhode Island, rarely attempted to play any controlling part in the political life of the community.

But with Massachusetts Bay the case was otherwise. There the colony came into existence full grown as a religious enterprise. There was no long period of slow development and ripening such as accompanied the rise of Virginia to the status of a colony. There was no dispatch of men of the rough-and-ready type, no ill-organized attempts at government for the preservation of order or the maintenance of peace, little serious quarreling or factional discord among the leaders, and for fifty-four years no successful interference from without to check or thwart the main purpose of the settlement. There were sickness, suffering, death, and disturbance, but never to such an extent as to endanger the continued prosperity of the settlement or the stability of its political system. Massachusetts was never a colony in the ordinary sense of the word; it was a Puritan commonwealth. In the seventeenth century it never fitted naturally into the way the English commercial and colonial scheme was working out, partly because it produced no staple that England wanted and therefore was of little economic value to the mother country, and partly because it resisted by every means in its power inclusion within the bounds of the expanding island kingdom and conformity to the rules which that kingdom laid down governing its relations with its colonies overseas.

Religion, always an accidental factor in promoting colonization anywhere, was the great impelling force that drove the Puritans to seek a refuge in the New World. It was the cohesive element that gave unity and strength to their life and organization in New England and held them together in loyalty to a common purpose. Religion was the tie that bound them all in an undeviating obedience to a peculiar regimen of life and conduct and fastened upon New England a form of churchly polity and rules of daily conduct that persisted for generations to follow. Religion circumscribed the Puritans' outlook, smothered their interest in a changing and progressive world, and centered their attention upon spiritual things as the chief concern of their existence.

These religious impulses had a noteworthy history behind them. In the life of the Western World from the fourteenth to the seventeenth centuries, two great movements were at work, which are called, in default of better terms, the Renaissance and the Reformation. One had to do with man's intellectual and cultural life, and so dealt with the things of this world; the other had to do with man's religious nature, and so concerned the things of the world to come. Both had something in common, for as the Renaissance went back to classical times for its standards of learning, beauty, and art, so the Reformation went back to the primitive days of the church for its ideas regarding ecclesiastical organization and religious worship. The Puritans, offspring of the latter movement, were in the main opposed to that which the Renaissance represented — humanism and the sensual side of life. They were not searching for purity of mind and body or for the improvement of the environment within which they lived; they were searching for purity of worship. They were interested not in things of this world, but in God and their own salvation, and they cultivated the humility that the sinner should feel in the presence of God. They had their eyes on the Hebraic past and the heavenly future and cared but little for purely material, physical, and intellectual matters except as means to a higher end. They paid very little attention to the idea that by taking thought they could add to the length of their years or to the comfort and earthly happiness of their fellow men. They took the world as they found it, a place of sin and temptation, and in their pilgrim's progress they met with little else than sorrow and trouble and endless labor. Life was but a probation that was ordained by God as a test of man's fitness for heaven. The real concern of man was the destiny of his soul. The future was all that really mattered; the heavenly home had many mansions and there the Puritan would find eternal rest.

The Puritanism which this description connotes, though dominant in New England for a century and a half, was an outstanding, articulate movement in England for only about fifty years, with Cromwell its last great political leader and Milton its last great poetical interpreter. With Cromwell died the influence of religion as a practical factor determining the direction and policy of government by "godly men"; and Milton's *Paradise Lost* is the swan song of the Puritan revolution, a poem untouched by the circumstances of the time when it was written—a presentation of Puritan theology cast in anthropomorphic form, a wonderfully imaginative and impressive picture of the divine purpose in Adam and the fall of man.

It is a significant and entirely consistent historical fact that during these years, when Puritanism was a contentious factor and a growing force in England, Massachusetts Bay was settled. That settlement was no mere manifestation of colonial enterprise. All the normal efforts at plantation in New England had thus far been unsuccessful, for the attempts which had been made at Sagadahoc, Wessagusett, and Cape Ann had all come to untimely ends, and only the small group of Pilgrims at Plymouth, itself in no sense a normal colony, had succeeded in fastening itself upon the soil. It required a greater incentive and a greater exercise of self-denial than gold and commercial profit furnished to overcome the hardships that all had to endure in that day for the establishment of permanent homes. That New England would have been settled eventually, just as Virginia and other colonies had been settled, had not the Puritans engaged in the great migration, no one can for a moment doubt, and had such settlement taken place it would have made a vast difference in the history of our country and in our country's historical literature. Massachusetts started already mature. Twenty thousand people came to New England in the first twelve years of her existence, founding a dozen or more towns along the shores of Massachusetts Bay and back, some of them, nearly thirty miles into the interior. They came to occupy a land where there had been before, besides the Pilgrims, hardly more than five hundred scattered adventurers, living isolated and independent lives devoted to fishing, fur trading, and a nomadic existence, without cohesion or organized government of any kind. Two hundred ships crossed the ocean in those years, bearing their cargoes of human souls for the populating of the territory of their selection, swayed by a religious conviction and purpose that held most of them harmoniously and unselfishly in devotion to a common cause. Religious conviction was not the only incentive that drove Pilgrim and Puritan to America, and peace and brotherly love were often absent from the Puritan communities and councils in the years that were to follow, but generally speaking it was the all-pervading faith in the religious rightness of their course and a dogmatic adherence to certain fundamental principles of government and ecclesiastical organization that gave to Massachusetts her strength and her superiority. The commonwealth thus set up, compacted and indurated by menacing dangers from without and enforced purifications from within, became a powerful homogeneous community that arrogated to itself the leadership of New England. Many of its members may have been indifferent or even apathetic, but the great majority were, either actively or passively, in accord with the conviction that governed the whole. They accepted the teachings of the elders and the laws of the magistrates and deputies, in things theological as well as secular, with no more murmuring than would be the case in any civil community. The Massachusetts colony of the seventeenth century was a Puritan state, powerful because of its numbers and of its wealth obtained through an early commercial expansion, but never losing its character as a settlement the design of which was religion. As time went on it passed through various stages of change and dissent in matters of doctrine as well as in views regarding government; but for the first fifty-four years of its history it was practically an independent religious commonwealth, representative of a single purpose – the erection of a City of God in the wilderness, in which God, not man, was to be served.

The movement that eventually brought the Puritans to New England began as a fishing venture, not unlike other fishing ventures of the day, promoted as early as 1622 by sundry merchants and adventurers of Dorchester in southwestern England. These men hoped to profit by setting up a plantation in the immediate neighborhood of the fish to be caught, thus saving both time and money by taking advantage of the proper season for fishing and cutting out the cost of extra seamen and the return of the fishing vessels to England. The originator of the idea and the leader among the adventurers was the Rev. John White, whom the historian Hubbard calls "one of the chief founders of the Massachusetts Bay Colony." The attempt failed and in 1626 the Dorchester company, "wearied of adventuring in that kinde by reason of their losses," withdrew its support and the Gloucester settlers dispersed. Some returned to England; others, moving southward under their manager, Roger Conant, took up land near what is now Salem. But not all of the Dorchester company were willing to give up the undertaking without further effort, and its most important member, the Rev. John White, did not despair. He hoped to make the place a religious refuge, not only for the fishermen along the coast, but also for those in England who were out of sympathy with the High-Church tendencies of the Anglican communion. These men, who represented the moderate wing of the Puritan movement in England, were eager to find a place for a settlement of their own, for they could not go to Plymouth where the Pilgrims had set up a church system based on a complete renunciation of the Church of England and all its works. At the same time there were others of similar ideas, though by no means the same ideas, to be found in Lincolnshire, East Anglia, and London, who believed with White that the principal object of such a colony should be religion. As a result, meetings were held in London, at which plans were made for the erection of a new company—the New England Company—to take over the Dorchester project and to plant a colony upon the place where Conant and the Old Planters were struggling, amid the hardships of a New England winter, to hold the group together.

The new company secured (as is commonly believed) a land patent from the Council for New England and, in June 1628, sent over John Endecott to reinforce the Conant settlement and to establish at Salem a plantation similar to that which the Virginia Company had founded at Jamestown twenty years before. But there was a good deal of uncertainty about land titles—for others had claims under the Council for New England to the very soil upon which the Salem plantation was located. Therefore, the Puritan leaders determined to place their enterprise on a sounder legal foundation and, notwithstanding the fact that the Council for New England had a prior title to the same territory by virtue of its charter of 1620, proceeded to go over the head of that council and themselves to obtain a confirmation of their patent in the form of a charter from the crown. This charter was finally issued on March 4, 1629, with the aid of Warwick and other influential men, and by it the New England Company was transformed into the Massachusetts Bay Company, an incorporated joint-stock company of the usual commercial type. This company was invested with the full powers of a trading and colonizing corporation, with rights of government and full title to the soil.

The circumstances attending the grant of this famous charter are far from easy to understand. In fact, the issue of all the patents of this period with which the Earl of Warwick's name is associated is so shrouded in mystery as to arouse doubts regarding the regularity of the proceedings. The land patent of 1628, the charter of 1629, and the Warwick patent of 1632 to the lords and gentlemen who planned to settle at Saybrook in Connecticut have all been the subject of controversy, largely because of the difficulty of obtaining satisfactory evidence about them. The territory of New England had already been granted to the Council for New England, and as far as the strictly legal rights of the case are concerned, the crown had no right to grant, or the New England Company to ask for, a charter conveying away power and titles that had already been conferred upon another duly incorporated company. This charter drove a wedge into the very heart of the region owned by the Council for New England and destroyed the unity of its possessions. What influences were brought to bear on the crown lawyers and the English officials can only be conjectured. The Council for New England was at the time inactive and almost moribund. Sir Ferdinando Gorges, its promoter and chief member, was involved in the war with France. On the other hand the Massachusetts Bay group had the coöperation of two powerful men at court — Lord Dorchester, one of the principal secretaries of state, and the Earl of Warwick, himself the titular president of the Council for New England, a

Puritan sympathizer, an active opponent of Gorges in all his enterprises, and a man keenly interested in privateering and colonization. It had also the assistance of two shrewd and energetic legal advisers, John White, the counselor, and Richard Bellingham of the New England Company, who had been recorder of the town of Boston in Lincolnshire and whom Israel Stoughton called "a great man and a lawyer." Lord Saye and Sele and Nathaniel Rich also helped the cause along. But these men, influential as they were, could hardly have brought about the desired result had there not been others of large wealth among the members of the company. Cradock, Saltonstall, Whetcombe, Venn, and Hewson were rich merchants of London, and Isaac Johnson was of the gentry with landed estates and property in the country. They were the ones who furnished the necessary funds and they must have drawn heavily upon their resources to meet what may charitably be called gratuities, fees, and legal expenses. It was said later (April 1629) that the charter had been obtained from his Majesty "with great cost, favor of personages of note, and much labor." That bribery was used we cannot affirm, for no two people are likely to agree on what constitutes a bribe. In this case it would have been necessary to buy over some important officials – such as the attorney-general and the secretary of state, not to mention privy councilors – a not impossible task, perhaps, but under any circumstances a difficult and expensive one. We know that the business was done with the utmost secrecy and circumspection, because it would have been fatal to the enterprise had news of what was being done been allowed to spread abroad. Probably no one would deny that the charter of the Massachusetts Bay Company was covertly and even "surreptiously" obtained.

The Massachusetts Bay Company was a trading company organized for the purpose of setting up in America a colony of its own. Its charter differed from that of the Virginia Company of 1612 only in language, being embellished with pious forms and phrases that were reverent and almost unctuous in tone, pointing to the desire of the petitioners to found a godly as well as a profit-making plantation. This plantation was to be governed from England in the usual fashion of plantations established in America by such English chartered corporations as the Virginia companies of London and Plymouth, created for both trade and colonization. But during the first six months of its history the Massachusetts Bay Company underwent a great and in some ways a momentous transformation. While pursuing its ordinary course as a trading corporation in England, nursing its infant colony at Salem and planning to develop its lands there by individual as well as by corporate means, it gradually came under the influence of a group of its own members that represented the most uncompromising and unyielding Puritan wing, for the Puritan movement was never uniform in all its parts. Its participants ranged from those who were conforming members of the Church of England but wished to purify the church from within rather than from without, to the nonconforming clergy and laity of the East Anglian region and elsewhere. The latter saw no hope in reform from within and believed that the only remedy lay in the establishment of a model community which by example should bring about the purification of the whole. These East Anglian Puritans, many of whom had interests in London, formed a close body of relatives and friends who were convinced that great calamities were about to fall upon England and that their only way to avoid these calamities was to leave their native country and erect a religious community in another place, which the Lord would choose for them, free from all earthly control except that of themselves. In the new world they felt they could carry out what they conceived to be the Lord's will, as from a study of the Bible and from the convictions of their own inner consciousnesses they understood that will to be. These men were so closely knit among themselves as to constitute a party, for their ideas and purposes were the same and their program of action was consistently adhered to. Their leader was John Winthrop, and among their number were Isaac Johnson, Emmanuel Downing, Thomas Dudley, and many others, not all of whom were at that time members of the company.

Beginning with a famous ride which Winthrop took with Emmanuel Downing, in July 1629, northward to Lincolnshire, to confer with the Earl of Lincoln, and with the signing of a compact known as the Cambridge Agreement of August 26 of that year, of which more will be said later, this group gradually took on organized form, ready for action. Already had the debates in the general court of the company shown the unmistakable presence there of two groups – the merchants and others representative of the more moderate Puritan views, who seemingly preferred that the company should remain in England, as it was originally intended to do, and pursue its course as a colonizing and trading body; and the East Anglians, men of determination and fixed religious resolve, with a clear-cut and, as they saw it, a divinely inspired program, who though not yet in the saddle were becoming more and more influential as the weeks passed.

Circumstances in the country at large were aiding their cause in making England an uncomfortable place to live in for the Puritans of the Winthrop type who found everything wrong in the world around them. Events within Parliament and without were forcing these men to consider seriously whether it were not better for them to turn their backs on England and seek residence elsewhere, and for that purpose to formulate a new scheme and plan of settlement. All the king's foreign policies had come to disastrous ends; the Protestant churches in Europe, menaced by the success of the imperial arms in the Thirty Years' War and not yet relieved by the victories of Gustavus Adolphus, were threatened with destruction. Parliament after two tempestuous sessions had been dissolved, with no promise of continuance; and the king, Charles I, who had been acclaimed with so much enthusiasm but four years before, was bringing only disappointment and gloom. A state of depression was spreading over the country, a plague was devastating the Continent and threatening England, grain was becoming scarce, unemployment was increasing, trade and industry — notably the cloth trade of the eastern-coast towns, due to the closing of the Spanish ports to English textiles in 1622 — were declining, poverty and distress, rioting and robbery were more prevalent than ever, and the government at that time (it did better afterward in the matter of poor relief) seemed powerless to check the disorder. The Star Chamber and the Court of High Commission were inflicting penalties upon those who broke the canons of the church or their ordination oaths; and while the hardships and injustices were less real than the Puritans thought them and the authority of courts and church was exercised without undue severity, the effect on the minds of Parliamentarian and Nonconformist alike was as profound as if both had become instruments of tyranny. Puritan ministers who refused to conform were silenced or deprived of their benefices, and some of them suffered in mind, body, and estate. Puritan writings were banned and burned, and probably some holding lesser offices under the government felt the weight of the royal displeasure, though I know of no certain case of such dismissal. The persecution of the Puritans in England under Charles I and Archbishop Laud has been greatly exaggerated and is not to be compared with that of the Waldenses in Piedmont, the Hu-

guenots in France, or even the Protestants under Queen Mary
or the Roman Catholics under Queen Elizabeth. We must
not forget that ears were cropped, noses slit, stocks and pillories made use of both in Virginia and Massachusetts, and
that at least one pernicious writing was burned in the latter
colony during the first half of the seventeenth century.

But inasmuch as England under these conditions was not a
place where a Nonconformist could live according to his
lights, this band of strong-minded, like-minded, positive men,
convinced of the rightness of their course and of the working
of God's spirit within them, determined on a far-reaching and
decisive step. They resolved to desert England and to go beyond the seas, out of the turmoil that surrounded them, and
far from the catastrophes that they thought were threatening
their native land. The decision was formally reached in the
Cambridge Agreement, already referred to, of August 26,
1629, signed by twelve men, not all of whom were members
of the company. The significance of this event lies not so much
in the agreement itself as in the effect of the agreement upon
the future of the company. Six of the signers brought the decision back to London and there it was debated in the general
court with no little difference of opinion. The idea of migration was in the air, but there were many views as to just what
ought to be done. Going to America did not necessarily mean
taking the company and the charter there too, for a plantation already existed at Salem to which Winthrop and the
others might have gone, leaving the company and the charter
in England. Why, therefore, did the men who signed the
agreement bind themselves to migrate only on condition that
"the whole Government, together with the patent," should be
allowed to go with them and to remain with them in the new
plantation overseas?

It is very much to be doubted whether the idea of transferring company and charter had been debated in the general court of the company before the return of these six men from Cambridge. The first form that the proposal took was not of so drastic a character. It went no farther than to agree that the local powers of the plantation might be increased so far as to make it to all intents and purposes a self-governing, independent community, as free as possible from interference on the part of the company in England. This is undoubtedly what Matthew Cradock meant when on July 28 he suggested that the government of the plantation be transferred "to those that shall inhabit there, and not to continue the same in subordination to the company heer, as now is." It must have taken a great deal of argument to persuade many of the original members of the company to consider seriously the transfer of the charter, for such a step was not only without precedent, but it was entirely foreign to the underlying purpose of this or any other trading company. Had such a plan been existent from the first and known to those responsible for the issue of the charter, it is wholly improbable that the charter would ever have passed the seals. Such an act meant the complete obliteration of the company as a trading corporation in England, a step of such doubtful legality that the signers at Cambridge agreed to it only in case it could be done legally and by order of the court of the company. The order of the court was obtained, but there is nothing to show that the legality of the transfer was ever determined. Probably to have done so would have broken the secrecy with which they wished to surround the whole transaction.

On August 29 the vote was taken in the general court of the company; and under pressure, no doubt, from those who had returned from Cambridge, a decision was reached in line with the Cambridge Agreement. From this time forward the Cambridge signers and those that were in accord with them obtained full control of the company's affairs. Their influence, hitherto more subtly and secretly expressed, now took open form in the election of John Winthrop as governor of the company in October 1629. The destiny of the company and charter was fixed—both were to go to New England, there to become the basis of an independent, self-governing Puritan state, free from all interference from outside, and itself exercising all the powers contained in the charter and such others, implied or not, as were necessary for the government of a commonwealth.

Why was this step taken and why in the mind of Winthrop and the others was such a step necessary? Why were they not willing to migrate, accepting increased powers from the company but leaving company and charter in England? Why were they not willing to become a colony such as Jamestown was, standing to the company in England as Jamestown stood to the Virginia Company? Such a colony might, equally well, have become a place of refuge, a home for God's oppressed people, and the seat of a model church, in which both polity and worship would be determined in Puritan fashion, as an example to the mother church of what such worship and polity ought to be. It is not easy to fathom the mysteries of human conduct when the reasons for such conduct have not been expressed in words, written down at the time and preserved. But I think that the explanation is not far to seek or difficult to understand. Winthrop, Dudley, Johnson, Saltonstall, Downing, and the rest believed that in order to carry out the divine purpose there should be erected in the New World—in such place as God should choose for his people—a Puritan church and state, within which might be made effective the will and plan of God. Such a church and state, they believed, would furnish an opportunity to apply Puritan ideas, based on the injunctions of the Bible, as to how life should be lived, worship conducted, government in church and state administered, God venerated, and his law obeyed. Such a community or commonwealth, call it what you will, was to have only one superior and that was God. To create such a state was Winthrop's mission. What Winthrop wanted, what he attempted to set up, and what he strove to the end of his life to maintain was a religious community, somewhere out of England in a country hitherto unoccupied, that should represent, not man's will and purpose, but that of God as far as he and his fellow Puritans could discover it, which in their profound convictions was very far indeed.

Winthrop reasoned, and from the point of view of his mission he reasoned rightly, that the Massachusetts Bay Company, like all joint-stock companies, was an open corporation; that is, any one purchasing its stock became a member and could vote at its meetings. As a result it might happen that in time the personnel of the company would change so as to be entirely out of sympathy with the Puritan plans as carried out in America. Something very like this actually did happen in the history of the Bermuda Company. Now, to leave the ultimate control over the colony in New England in the hands of a company in England that might eventually become indifferent or even hostile or might possibly have its charter taken away, thus throwing the colony into the hands of the crown, was to allow God's purpose to be thwarted by the intervention of man. The only way to prevent this disaster was to get rid of the company in England, and to Winthrop's ingenious mind (or to the ingenious mind of some one else) that could be done most easily by taking company and charter along with them to New England, thus swallowing up the company in the colony. In this way the company would be under Puritan control and could be manipulated to serve Puritan ends, which, as Winthrop argued, were the ends of God.

But the company in England was not the only secular authority that the Puritans needed either to get rid of by absorption or to ward off by the best logic at their command. They tried to eliminate the king and his executive officials by insisting that the latter, in approving the grant of the charter, had divested themselves of all right to interfere in the affairs of the colony, a manifest piece of sophistry since the charter was not granted for any such purpose. They threw off the authority of Parliament by asserting that the statute law of England did not concern them, partly because they had no representation at Westminster and consequently did not share in the making of laws, and partly because English statute law did not pass beyond the four seas and so had no force in America. They set aside as unimportant the pretensions, which they had already flouted, of the Council for New England because they believed that actual possession was nine points of the law and that the council would never be able to recover its title either by force or by any legal process. Neither one of these arguments would have been of any avail had conditions been different in England, but the troubles which came upon that kingdom in the years from 1630 to 1660 made it possible for Massachusetts to intrench herself firmly in New England and to commit many acts of aggressiveness and doubtful legality when strictly construed from the standpoint of English colonization and English law. The fact that the Puritan state in New England in no way conformed to the status of a regular and normal colony, but rather endeavored to make of itself something that was foreign to the fundamental idea of what a colony should be and to what England expected it to be, led to a great deal of trouble afterward. It was inevitable that all sorts of difficulties should arise and friction be engendered in the efforts of the Puritans to erect an independent religious community on land that was the property of the English king and within the scope of his legitimate control. Two points of view could hardly be wider apart than that of the Puritans, obeying what they believed to be the commands of God, overriding all claims that the king might make to authority over them, and that of the public officials of England, influenced not by any obligation to obey the Lord's will but by the laws, customs, and needs of the kingdom.

One cannot read Puritan records and literature for the half century from 1630 to 1684 without realizing that the relations of the Massachusetts commonwealth with England were shaped at all times by this overshadowing fear of outside political control. The Puritans wished to be left alone to work out their own salvation in their own way, but that was not to be, for always in the eyes of the English authorities they were a colony, subject to such control as England had a right to exercise outside the limitations of its charter. Should they go beyond the bounds of their charter, as they were certain to do in the effort to erect a separate, independent, self-governing state, they were liable to incur the penalty of such unauthorized encroachments and to suffer the loss of their palladium of liberty, as they did eventually in 1684. The history of those fifty years is one long effort on their part to ward off the blow that finally came. The Puritans were always afraid that a governor general might be appointed over them, though that fear was not realized until the days of Andros. They resisted with all the means at their command the threatened intervention in 1635, when Sir Ferdinando Gorges and his allies actually obtained a writ of quo warranto against them and when more favorable circumstances in England might have ended the Puritan experiment then and there. They refused to obey the orders and commissions of the Long Parliament, lest in so doing they should establish a precedent that might endanger their liberty by implying that they could do nothing but by authority out of England. They gave only lip service to the king after the Restoration and fought by every means at their disposal – disobedience, procrastination, and misunderstanding – to avoid the inevitable absorption of their state into the expanding English commercial and colonial empire. And just as the Puritan magistrates sought to prevent the outside and alien world from breaking in upon their independence and impairing the perfection of their system, so they labored within, by persuasion, persecution, and banishment, to prevent any modification or abatement of the principles upon which their system was based. They drove out Anglican, Antinomian, Anabaptist, and Quaker, and others "not fit to inhabit here," and they opposed the extension of the franchise, any decrease in their own power, any increase in the power of the deputies, and the elimination of the elders as political advisers – all because they did not believe in a democracy or in any form of popular government and were afraid that the principles upon which the City of God in Massachusetts was founded would be menaced from within as well as from without.

All these precautions were taken in defense of what Winthrop and the other magistrates believed to be a divinely ordained work and in order to maintain intact and unchanged a form of polity, worship, faith, and morals that found their justification in their religious convictions. I believe that these elder Puritan statesmen (if we can call them statesmen) were convinced that to allow intervention from without and modification from within was to be guilty of sin; and that many a Puritan's exhibition of blind stupidity, harshness, inhumanity, and even cruelty, all of which some are inclined to condemn far too readily, was due to his endeavor to live up to what he believed was the will, or feared was the wrath, of God. These phrases have played a very large part in the history of the world, and the first, used as a battle cry since the days of Peter

the Hermit, has driven men to commit deeds that can be satisfactorily explained on no other ground than a mistaken sense
of religious duty. To the Puritans, God's will was unchanging, his system was fixed, and his commands were imperative.
Their scheme of theology admitted no law of progress, no
alteration in the divine plan of rewards and punishments.
Living for the world to come and adhering to an unalterable
creed, polity, and rule of conduct, they ignored, in their ab-
sorbing interest in the great work of the soul's salvation, many
of the stubborn facts of earthly existence. They maintained a
strict code of moral behavior that gave very little leeway to the
frailties of the ordinary man. Wherever Puritan rule was enforced, whether in Massachusetts, New Hampshire, or Maine,
the lord brethren kept constant watch over morals and conduct.
They had on hand a long list of indictable offenses – some to
be corrected at home and in church and others to be dealt with
in the town and county courts – such as immorality, debt, tres-
pass, breach of covenant or contract, slander, assault, swearing,
and blasphemy, punishable by fines, flogging, confinement in
stocks and pillories, and other contrivances for bringing the
sinner to repentance. Laziness and vagabondage were placed
under the ban and suffering and endurance were extolled as
virtues beyond reproach. The graces of life were so many
snares of the devil. The more the Puritans endured, the more
they believed the Lord would approve of them. But art, music,
profane literature, and science in any modern sense of the
word were repudiated as corrupting the flesh and impeding
the divine purpose. By flogging and suppressing human weak-
nesses, the Puritans in Massachusetts of the seventeenth century tried to keep themselves in the straight and narrow way,
but inevitably, in the long run, human nature asserted itself
and the normal balance had to be restored. Politically, also,
the ever-widening circle of British expansion surrounded them

and in the end the Puritan commonwealth fell, as it had to fall, as an independent state, and became, what it did not want to be, a colony in regular standing under the British crown. But even then it was less of a normal colony than was Virginia, because a charter – the charter of 1691 – intervened between it and the royal will. Not until 1775 did Massachusetts become a typical colony under the king's direct control.

Manifestly it was impossible that isolation from all contact with the outside world could be maintained by men who lived on the shores of such a favorable harbor as that of Boston, in which contemporaneously it was estimated that five hundred vessels could ride at anchor in good depth of water. In fact, during the second decade a mercantile and commercial activity began that was destined to have a profound effect upon Puritan history and to play an important part in breaking down the barriers of seclusion. The Puritans may have eschewed the frivolities of mind and heart, but they had a keen regard for land and the profits of industrial and financial enterprise, and, as has been well said, they were able to harmonize the quest of profit with the quest of God. After 1642, shipbuilding and commerce became the leading interests of Boston, Charlestown, Dorchester, and Salem, and vessels as small as twelve tons for coastwise service and as large as four hundred tons for ocean-going voyages gradually effected a transformation in the outward appearance of these maritime towns by making them the centers of wealth and a new prosperity. The days when the Puritans were reduced to a diet of acorns, clams, and Indian corn were gone never to return, and all classes of the population – to an extent they had never experienced in old England – were clothed, housed, and fed comfortably. At no time, after the first few years, was there any poverty or beggary in the Massachusetts colony under Puritan rule.

Until about 1640 the colony was essentially a place of agricultural activity, but at that time began an era of commercial enterprise that was to continue throughout the colonial period. Vessels went up and down the coast as far north as Newfoundland and as far south as Virginia. Overseas they went to England, Ireland, Holland, France, Portugal, Spain, into the Mediterranean to Italy and Syria, and even to the Guinea coast and the Wine Islands. With the West Indies their contacts were frequent and profitable. Increased labor in the fields and farms produced a surplus of salable commodities, and trips to the fishing waters of the North gave them a supply of cod, herring, and mackerel which they exchanged for cash or commodities with the Roman Catholic countries of the Continent. Boston became a distributing center for manufactured goods from abroad and its imports during these years enable us to picture the Puritans of that day as enjoying no little abundance and luxury.

During these years the Massachusetts fathers were endeavoring by every means in their power to preserve the ecclesiastical polity and discipline of the founders from unorthodox contamination; they were struggling with the problem of how to stretch the terms of a trading company's charter to meet the needs of a growing commonwealth – a feat which they manifestly could not perform and soon ceased to contend with; and the people in their towns were widening the area of supply and increasing the agricultural output for the purpose of furnishing materials for export. Meanwhile, the merchants, sea captains, and mariners were extending their trading opportunities into all parts of the north Atlantic, were adding to the gross wealth of the colony, and were raising to a level beyond the dreams of the first immigrants the standards of dress, furnishing, and food. Though it was to be a long time before these conditions seriously affected the political and religious convictions of the Puritan magistrate, they did increase his confidence, aggressiveness, and pride, because their very success seemed to him a witness to God's protecting care. He argued that as long as God was with him and was manifesting approval by the well-being vouchsafed to him, man should not be afraid. The growing affluence of the commonwealth served to strengthen him in his adherence to all that pertained to the covenant, membership, and discipline of the church; and at the same time stiffened him in his determination to resist as long as possible any attempt on England's part to limit the scope of his trading facilities. So hopeful was he that he was unable to foresee the inevitable consequences of a continued and obstinate refusal to conform to the requirements of England's colonial policy.

There is something extraordinarily interesting from the standpoint of human psychology in the mental outlook of many of these men – Winthrop, Dudley, and Endecott of the earlier generation and Danforth, Nowell, and Oakes of the later – who were unable to square the purposes of God in the world with the normal desires of everyday men in the everyday walks of life; and one cannot but look with wonder upon their belief in the last days of the Puritan era that God would interpose to save his people and by some form of miraculous intervention preserve them against the power of Satan. They stood, as they themselves said, "in need of the help of Heaven" and they waited for that help from heaven to the bitter end.

It has been customary in the past to extol the political and social principles of the Puritans as of great significance, as if they anticipated the doctrines which were destined to become in time the warp and woof of our American system of government. I doubt this. I doubt if in the writings of Winthrop or of any of the Massachusetts leaders of the seventeenth century can be found anything to warrant such laudation. The Puritans were not utopians or dreamers; they were hard-headed, practical politicians of their own kind, and nowhere in their writings or their applications of policy can be found any generalizations foreshadowing the ideals of the later American republic. They were none of them philosophers, theorists, or speculators. They were realists in every sense of the word and at bottom theological realists, in that their every thought and action had a religious end in view. None of them would have subscribed to our American doctrines regarding church and state, popular government, or religious freedom. The bases of Winthrop's political thought were the overruling sovereignty of God, the natural inevitableness of the inequality of man, and the essentially autocratic organization of society, arising out of nature, order, and antiquity. Winthrop condemned democracy, equality, toleration, and the separation of church and state, denied free speech in principle as well as in fact, abhorred opposition in government, and believed that it was for the good of the people to vest all power in the hands of those most competent to exercise it. He took the ground that true liberty lay in subjection to authority and that the authority of the magistrates was of divine origin, even though the men themselves might have been elected by the freemen of the colony. Such political dicta find no response in the mind of the modern American. No one can defend Winthrop as a great political thinker, however much we may respect his character, and no one can find in the early Massachusetts system a model society for the world of today. In the struggles of the deputies for more authority and of the nonfreemen for more privileges, we can find a phase of that larger movement towards an increase of control in the hands of those that have it not – a movement that has been going on since the beginning of time. But the Puritan magistrate in Massachusetts fought that movement as long as he could and only gave in when he had to. The consent of the people as a whole had no place in the political philosophy of the Massachusetts Puritan.

Why was it that the Puritans were able to establish this remarkable state in New England and so to buttress it as to give it continuance for fifty-four years? The explanation is simple and is to be found in the circumstances of the time. From 1630 to 1660 England was in a condition of turmoil and disturbance. Note the sequence of events: arbitrary rule by Charles I, financial bankruptcy, revolt of the Short and Long Parliaments, civil wars, execution of the king, and rule of the Puritan minority in England for eleven years. This entire breaking down of the customary administrative and executive powers in England and the dominance of a party favorable to Massachusetts explains why the Puritans were enabled to set up in Massachusetts a form of government that was an anomaly in the history of English colonization. The rise of Massachusetts to the position of an independent commonwealth exercising all the prerogatives of sovereignty was due to the ascendancy of the Puritans in England, an ascendancy that the Puritans of Massachusetts ascribed in all sincerity to the intervention of God. During the civil wars, the opponents of the Puritans in New England were drawn off from any further attempts to establish claims to territory in the New World; and during the period that followed, when Cromwell and the English Puritans were in command, Massachusetts was left undisturbed to carry out to the full the plans of her leaders. She extended her jurisdiction over New Hampshire and Maine; she coined money and created corporations, neither of which she had any legal right to do; and she established her own commercial system and adhered to it in spite of the different system which the mother country was gradually bringing into existence. She did this with all the confidence and assertiveness of a state free, independent, and sovereign. The day of reckoning came with the restoration of the king, Charles II, in 1660, and in the subsequent inquiry that followed into the affairs of the colony, an inquiry that finally ended with the annulment of the charter in 1684.

It is one thing to extol those qualities of mind and character that have given to the Puritan inheritance its distinctive place in the history of our country, but it is quite another thing to defend the Puritan commonwealth as a model state, unjustly and illegally overthrown. It would not be difficult to defend the opposite thesis – that the commonwealth itself existed illegally from the beginning, and that the annulment of its charter was justified, not only because of the illegalities practised under its protection but also because of the illegality of its very being from the standpoint of English law, to which the Puritans in Massachusetts were subject as well as the king's subjects at home. What I want to say, as I approach my conclusion, is that to have preserved (had that been possible) the religious doctrines of the Puritans, as shaped in the seventeenth century, to have perpetuated their ideals of government as worked out in the days of Winthrop and Dudley, and to have continued a polity based on what these men conceived was God's will in his relations to men would have served no good ends either for Massachusetts or the world at large. The experiment is one of great fascination, deserving of fair-minded and intelligent observation. No one can but respect the men who took part in it, burdened as they were by the weight of their convictions and narrowed by their own dwarfed and cramped outlook on life. They suffered and endured, struggled and fought, but in their abnormal interest in the problems of sin and salvation they allowed many of the finer traits of man's nature to become atrophied. It is no part of the historian's duty to pass judgment upon them. They failed in their immediate end, the permanent establishment of a City of God in the wilderness; but they did not fail in the training of men or in establishing many noteworthy principles of conduct and government which they handed on to later generations.

Massachusetts, unlike Virginia, started, as it were, full grown, with a life that was singularly uniform in all its parts—in the organization of its towns, in the manifold varieties of its agricultural products, in the diversified nature of its commercial connections, in the rigidity of its ecclesiastical structure and discipline, and in the quality and interests of its people. Instead of accepting the status of a colony, as did Virginia after 1624, recognizing the authority over them of the executive and legislative authorities in England, the Puritans deliberately cut themselves off from the official control of their mother country, denying the right of both crown and Parliament to concern themselves with their affairs. They interpreted their charter as a protection against England but not as a final guide to their own conduct, transgressing its terms and overstepping its bounds whenever they felt it was necessary to do so. Though they could not free themselves entirely from the influence of English law and not at all from personal contact with the homeland, they did so outwardly in their official acts, in their land law and law of descent, and after 1652 introduced into their deeds the phrase "according to the manner and custom [not of old England but] of New England." They followed their own bent in many features of their administrative system and in the organization of their churches after the "New England Way." They were never viewed with favor in old England, where they were looked upon as a recalcitrant people, obstinately adhering to an entire freedom of action in things political, legal, and commercial, the most prejudicial of all the plantations to the kingdom of England. Consequently, the effort to bring Massachusetts into line with the other colonies probably cost the mother country more trouble, debate, and controversy, and provided opportunity for more recrimination and ill will than was the case with all the other colonies put together. We extol, and rightly, the virtues of the Puritans and respect a certain steadfastness and tenacity of purpose, sense of responsibility, devotion to conscience, and power of endurance for righteousness' sake that have given them an enviable place in history, and we can understand the circumstances of their origin and the reasons which determined their attitude towards their mother country, but we cannot in all honesty sympathize with their principles of government or with the objects they sought to attain in seeking the erection of an independent Puritan state in the wilderness of New England.

IV

RHODE ISLAND: THE TROUBLED HOME
OF SOUL LIBERTY

RHODE ISLAND is the smallest State in the Union, having an area but forty miles square, of which about one seventh is water surface and the remainder a soil that is not well adapted for agricultural purposes. This mite of a State, sometimes called a spangle instead of a star, was composed at the beginning of many separate companies of sensate and intelligent beings, each group of which struggled into existence under various auspices and impulses. For the first century of their history the peoples that made up these companies spent time, energy, and patience in the effort to cement and consolidate their scattered communities into a working union that should represent a common loyalty. With them as with all peoples who have created federal unions out of detached and independent parts the end was attained only as the result of pressure and necessity.

Rhode Island was a wilderness—a barbarous and howling wilderness—when the first settlers entered it and continued to remain so for many generations to come. The colony was not settled directly from England but in largest part by overflow from Massachusetts and Connecticut. It is a significant fact that the Puritan colony of Massachusetts Bay, in its effort to serve its God and to preserve its orthodoxy in both church and state, lost some of its ablest and most intelligent men and women and in so doing undoubtedly weakened its influence in New England, great though that influence was. Had Massachusetts been more lenient and less uncompromising she might have accomplished more, both in extending her political authority and widening her territory. If she had not allowed her religious convictions to override her good sense, she might have become the mother of colonies and have carried her jurisdiction to the north and west and south, instead of losing territory, as was actually the case, in every direction. But she drove out Roger Williams and Anne Hutchinson of Rhode Island, John Wheelwright and John Underhill of New Hampshire; vented her wrath upon Samuel Gorton of Rhode Island; and made it impossible for William Coddington of Rhode Island, Thomas Hooker, John Haynes, and Roger Ludlow of Connecticut, William Pynchon of Springfield, and John Davenport of New Haven to remain. In her boundary disputes with Connecticut, Rhode Island, and New Hampshire she lost in the end nearly everything that she tried to obtain. Thus, instead of becoming the protector of New England and the guardian of her weaker neighbors, she surrounded herself with a group of hostile or at least unfriendly settlements, a condition that made rather for disunity and ill will than for unity and coöperation. No one outside her own boundaries really liked her or approached her with sentiments of affection and sympathy. Except during the rule of the Puritan minority in England, the authorities abroad viewed her with misgiving and a rising dissatisfaction that culminated in the loss of her charter and the ending of her career as an independent Puritan commonwealth. But nowhere, whether in England or New England, was the bitterness against her so poignant or prolonged as it was in Rhode Island. Massachusetts historians (Professor Channing, for example) may wonder that the histories of Rhode Island are so full of prejudice against Massachusetts, but the cause goes back to the beginnings of the colony and is inwrought in the very nature of the policy that Massachusetts pursued in the seventeenth century of turning against her, in a greater or lesser degree, all those who did not think or act as she did.

Roger Williams was banished from Massachusetts in 1635, not because he advocated soul liberty or liberty of conscience – for the controversy over that subject did not begin until the days of the Long Parliament in England – but for other and equally important reasons. He denied the validity of the Massachusetts Bay charter and the right of the king to grant lands that he did not justly own. He abhorred the Massachusetts view of incomplete separation from the Church of England, declaring that the separation should be absolute, not only from the English church as a national body but also from each parish church taken by itself, a view which the Puritan clergy of New England refused to countenance. He declared that the power of the civil magistrate extended only to the bodies, goods, and outward estate of men and not to offenses against the spiritual law, a charge that he developed in his later writings, involving the principle of soul liberty. This principle was given legal warrant and royal protection in the charter of 1663, which stipulated that no person should be molested for any differences of opinion that he might have in matters of religion. Thus it became the law and practice of colony and state that all men should have freedom to worship God unmolested by the civil authorities and exempt from all taxation for the support of any other man's religion, a rule from which Rhode Island has never deviated. The establishment of this principle may well be called Roger Williams's great gift to the nation.

These settlers of Rhode Island, who later spoke of themselves as "poor despised peasants that lived remote in the woods," were a heterogeneous collection of men and women who held many sorts of religious and social opinions, and who sought a refuge there for conscience' sake and other reasons, because they were unable to live anywhere else. They were fugitives from other places where they were not wanted, and, while divided in their own ideas of life and government, were at one in their antagonism to the Puritan rule of Massachusetts, from which they wished to separate themselves as far as possible. Rhode Island's colonial problem was, therefore, how to create a single commonwealth out of these multifarious and discordant elements.

Unlike the people of Massachusetts and Connecticut, these inhabitants of the Rhode Island communities had no common faith or church polity, no common set of opinions or beliefs, no common religious practices enforced by law. They recognized no standing religious order of any kind, for each individual or family followed its own peculiar bent, and groups of individuals or families came together each under its own particular form of church worship. There were even those in the various settlements who deemed it against their conscience to be bound by any law, human or divine, and were bitterly opposed to the idea of a state church and a settled clergy, an attitude that always prevailed in colonial Rhode Island and continued to prevail in some parts of the State well on into the nineteenth century. This was inevitable with a people who were offshoots, not of the Puritans in England, but rather of the more radical groups there, such as Antinomians, Anabaptists, Familists, Generalists, rigid Separatists, and even libertines and anarchists. Among such people there could be neither political nor religious harmony, and even Roger Williams, the seeker and lover of peace, could view many of the activities of Anabaptists, Quakers, and libertines as attempts to break down the fundamental liberties of the community, which, as he said, should be "dearer than our right eyes."

Rhode Island was without any fixed or settled form of government until after 1647, when the patent of 1644 was put into operation and there was finally established for the first time a fairly centralized body of institutions possessing the prestige of mastery and authority. Even after the coming of the charter in 1663, the boundary lines were so long in dispute that no one living along them was quite sure where his allegiance lay. For a settlement occupying so small an area of territory, Rhode Island had to fight longer and harder for the little land she possessed than any other of the thirteen colonies. She was always afraid during these early years lest she should be pushed off into the sea by her troublesome neighbors, Massachusetts, Plymouth, and Connecticut. As one of her governors wrote, "we are in constant fear of the envious and subtle contrivances of our neighbor colonies round about us [who are] united in combination together to swallow us up." For thirty of her formative years she stood with her back to the ocean battling for existence, not only against encroachments upon her territory but (again to quote from a Rhode Island document) against "those incredible oppressions wee endured, of scorne and contempt, slander and reproach, threatenings and molestations, captiving and imprisoning, fining and plundering the people of this colonie" in the effort of the members of the New England Confederation "to roote us up and expose us to ruine." Inevitably such an experience in the days of her infancy left indelible marks upon her character as a people and the course of her history.

As if these troubles from without were not enough, there were always persons within the colony in the seventeenth century who were willing to work for the disintegration of the territory and to transfer their allegiance to other governments than their own. There was prolonged quarreling over land titles, forms of government, and payment of taxes and assessments. There were the activities of those whom Williams called "Aposers of all Authority," ringleaders strongly suspected of "contempt of the order of the colony," fomenters of faction and division, and everywhere those who opposed a strong executive and centralized control. Separatism, decentralization, and watchful waiting have been the proclivities that actuated Rhode Island's people in their own government and in their relations with each other and the rest of the world. Resistance to any form of encroachment upon her local independence has been a very axiom of her existence. Just as the townspeople never liked interference from the magistrates in matters of personal conduct and just as the towns did not like interference from the central government in whatever concerned their own affairs, so the State has never liked interference on the part of any higher authority outside itself. For instance, it refused to send delegates to the Federal Convention of 1787 and declined to ratify the Federal Constitution and many of its amendments, including the eighteenth, for the repeal of which the people of Rhode Island have recently voted.

Rhode Island at the beginning was formed of four separate and independent communities—Providence, Portsmouth, Newport, and Warwick—and we may even add a fifth, for Pawtuxet was at one time a distinct community. Each of these was founded by peoples of strong personalities and marked differences of opinion, and each was in embryo a petty sovereign state. Each possessed no other than an Indian title to its lands, and each had only a sort of agreement or social compact among its members as the basis and legal warrant for its government. Each recognized the king of England as its sovereign and acknowledged its subordination to the law and authority of the mother country. In the first half century five men stand out conspicuously in the colony's affairs and dominate them: William Coddington of Newport, Samuel Gorton of Warwick, Dr. John Clarke of Newport, William Harris of Providence, and Roger Williams of Providence, who belonged in a sense to the whole colony.

Coddington was a man of wealth, education, political

shrewdness, and business capacity. He made Newport, which he founded in 1639, the starting point in Rhode Island's great commercial development, so that for more than a century Newport was Rhode Island and with its ships ploughed the sea until it became the richest and most progressive of all the towns in the colony. In his earlier years Coddington, ambitious to become a state-maker, schemed to erect his island into a kind of feudal propriety, of which he should be the lord and master and the people his tenants. In this, as we shall see, he failed. Later in life he turned Quaker, and abandoning the garb of a man of the world donned the drab costume of the Society of Friends. Newport after 1670 became the seat of the Quaker rule in Rhode Island.

Samuel Gorton, who founded Warwick, was an eccentric character whose early writings on theological questions are so involved that even the most patient reader had difficulty in understanding them. He formulated his own theological ideas, which were personal and not those of a sect, stood for liberty of conscience and the denial of the power of the civil government to interfere with spiritual things, and was vehemently opposed to the formalities and perfunctory worship of the churches. He was a firm believer in the binding force of the common law of England and in the authority of the English government, and refused to recognize the validity of the magistracy in Boston, Plymouth, and Portsmouth or to acknowledge the legality of the New England courts. Unlike Williams he was profoundly convinced of the efficacy of charters. He had much in his theology that was similar to the teachings of Mrs. Hutchinson, but he disagreed with her as he did with the Quakers in their doctrine of Christ and the inner light because he was not convinced of the value of emotionalism. He was not a Trinitarian, viewing the Trinity as but three manifestations of the nature of Christ, and he would have nothing to do with the conventional universities and schools, because he preferred "the universitie of human reason and the reading of the great volume of visible creation." He followed no man's thinking but developed a theology that was peculiar to himself. In some ways he was a good deal of a modern.

Dr. John Clarke, who obtained the charter of 1663, was a physician and preacher of Newport, forming what Cotton Mather called "the Angelic Conjunction," combining the cure of the body with the cure of the soul. He helped Coddington found Newport, was one of those responsible for the union of Newport and Portsmouth in 1640, and from that time to 1651, when he went to England, was a leader in the affairs of the colony. His mission abroad called for patience, tact, unimpeachable honesty, and loyalty to the colony, the interests of which he was called upon to serve. He suffered for his devotion, as the expense of his mission was more than the colony could bear at the time, and he was obliged to mortgage his house and lands at Newport for cash to go on with until the colony could raise the necessary funds, which it finally did with difficulty. Next to Roger Williams no man stands higher in the esteem of Rhode Island than does this faithful and efficient public servant.

William Harris, the so-called anarchist, malcontent, and litigant, and the one man that Roger Williams distinctly did not like, was a turbulent soul, possessed of considerable knowledge of English law and legal procedure and unquestioned business shrewdness, sometimes of a dubious sort. He was amazingly active in mind, with a habit of frequently changing his opinions, both religious and political — a habit which bore witness to the unrest and discontent that raged within him. He was given to controversy and was tenaciously persistent in his determination to obtain what he considered were his honest rights, particularly in matters of land. He spoke of himself as a "long and great sufferer" and a "weary traveller for the space of almost forty years in the wilderness of New England." Though he denied the right of the state to limit the sovereignty of man, he was not the "damnable villain and impudent morris dancer" that his enemies called him in language that was often violent and inflammatory, for he had many redeeming qualities, won the confidence of men in England and Rhode Island, and was successful in nearly all his suits at law. It is unfortunate that some of the leading men in Rhode Island and elsewhere in our colonial history are best known and judged by the fervors and indiscretions of youth rather than by the riper wisdom of more mature years.

Roger Williams never really systematized his ideas. He evidently did his thinking and meditating during his many lonely wanderings among the Indians, or while he bent over the hoe as he cultivated his fields or laboriously plied the paddle as he passed up and down the rivers or made his way across the more perilous waters of Narragansett Bay. After 1640 he directed his attention in considerable part to problems of government as well as religion. His first great work in this field, the *Bloudy Tenent*, as well as others that followed after, stripped of their verbiage, are treatises on political science as well as theology. They deal with government in church and state, with the principles that should control life and conduct, and with the problems of peace, arbitration, education, and the general welfare of the individual and the community. His fundamental theses may be very briefly stated. He viewed the church not as an integral part of the state, with the ends identical and the individuals its servants—as did Massachusetts, Connecticut, New Haven, and the Puritans generally—but as one of the many civil corporations that the state was bound to protect. Hence arose his ideas of liberty of conscience and the separation of church and state. He willingly conceded that the civil magistrate was superior in place, honors, dignities, and earthly powers, but insisted that the church was superior ecclesiastically, should be entirely free from magisterial interference, and was possessed of authority to rule the magistrates in a church way. This idea of the separation of church and state he couched in a great variety of phrases and supported with a great variety of arguments.

Williams went far beyond toleration, assuming a position diametrically opposed to that of the Massachusetts leaders, who took the ground that no other church, practising another form of church discipline, could be approved as having a right to exist in the colony. Cotton Mather put the matter well when he said, at a later time, that if "the discipline which we here practice be (as we are persuaded of it) the same which Christ hath appointed and therefore unalterable, we see not how another can be lawful, and therefore if a company of people shall come hither and here set up and practice another we pray you think not much, if we cannot promise to approve of them in so doing." Roger Williams would have none of this doctrine, for he believed that the world was full of admirable people – men and women – who not only thought differently from himself in church polity and organization, but who might not be Christians at all. In his famous metaphor of the ship going to sea, which he introduced into his letter to Providence in 1655, he included in his "true picture of a commonwealth" Papists, Protestants, Jews, and Turks, all of whom had the right not only to be tolerated but to live and worship in their own way. They were not to be "forced," as he expressed it, "to come to the ship's prayers or worship nor compelled from their own particular prayers, if they practice any." Thus he stood not for toleration but for absolute equality as far as liberty of conscience was concerned. At the same time he was ready to enter into arguments on theological questions, as he did for three days with the Quakers at Newport and Providence in 1672, a debate that led to the issue of the pamphlet, *George Fox digg'd out of his Burrowes* which is a narrative of this disputation, and to which Fox replied in *A New England Fire-Brand Quenched*, presenting the Quaker version.

Thus, to Williams the state was a purely civil concern, external in its administration, internal in the minds of men, wholly unconcerned with spiritual matters. He accepted the idea of the social compact, but interpreted it in the light of a community-consciousness of a common purpose. To him the state was a commonweal of families agreeing to live together for the common good – a body of people who had fundamentally in themselves the source of power to select what governors and government they agreed on. The state was not a religious community, for Williams rejected totally the divine origin of government and the divine character of the magistracy, upon which Massachusetts laid so much stress. He profoundly believed, as he said, that kings and magistrates had no more power than the people "betrusted" them with. This point he returns to over and over again in his writings. "The sovereign power of all civil authority is founded in the consent of the people"; "the sovereign, original, and foundation of civil power lies in the people ... and if so a people may erect what form of government seems to them most mete for their civil condition"; "such governments have no more power nor for a longer time than the civil power or people consulting and agreeing shall betrust them with"; and again, "the sovereign power of all civil authority is founded in the consent of the people." In all this he is anticipating a future day such as the present, when sovereignty was to get lodged in the mass of the people, and when for the first time in the history of governments great bodies of men were to be consciously in control of affairs. He distinguished carefully between civil power,

which lay in the people of the community, and civil government, which was the exercise of authority by those whom the
people elected for that purpose.

Williams's idea of individualism was not that of an isolated
individualism but rather one that found its highest expression
through the enforcement of law and the limitation of individual activities. To him freedom was not the ability to do as
one pleased but a privilege acquired by him who was one of a
social group, in which the individual had duties as well as
rights. This linking of rights and duties, which oddly enough
is not to be found in our own Federal Constitution and appears for the first time in the history of constitution-drafting
in the French constitution of 1792, was very much on Williams's mind and often in his speech and was given a kind of
statutory form in the Rhode Island acts and orders of 1647.
Williams opposed the individualist William Harris of Providence, not only because of the latter's land claims, but even
more because Harris adhered to the Generalist doctrine of un-
restrained individualism, was inclined to controversy rather
more than most of the strange aggregation of individuals in
that settlement, and held views quite unlike those of Williams
on the rights of man and the duties of citizenship. Harris
made a public avowal of "anarchy" and in so doing brought
upon himself the charge of treason, for he contended that he
"who can say 'it is his conscience' ought not to yield subject to
any human order amongst men." This, to Williams, was a refusal to distinguish between liberty and license, a difference, it
must be said, that was never very clearly comprehended by a
large number of the early settlers of Rhode Island.

The views thus entertained by Roger Williams, as well as
those entertained by Thomas Hooker of Connecticut and William Penn of Pennsylvania, were utopian in their application
to a living society. These men conceived of a community de-

liberately controlled by human reason and intelligence; they imagined a social order carefully planned and managed without much regard for its background of habit and experience; and they thought it would be possible to erect a government that would be responsive to the sovereign power – the people – from which it derived its authority. None of these conditions prevailed anywhere in the world in the seventeenth and eighteenth centuries and hardly anywhere in the nineteenth. Can we say that these conditions prevail in practice even today? These men conjured up a vision of an ideal body of people, such as never was in the history of man. They dreamed of a world where freedom, equality, individualism, coöperation, and harmony should be the guides of conduct, and it is not surprising that they should have seen their hopes shattered or needing to be greatly modified when brought face to face with the stern realities of human nature. They took no account of the vested interests of individuals or corporate groups or of the peculiarities of towns and sections, and completely ignored the thousand and one influences that are always at war with efforts to promote the common good. Circumstance was to prove too much for Roger Williams; and in the issue, Rhode Island was to prove no more of a peaceful or harmonious fellowship than was the settlement which William Penn started on the banks of the Delaware fifty years later to prove a place of brotherly love. Each was to see his scheme torn and rended and each was to cry out against the brutishness of his fellow men. Williams had a magnificent faith and even when living, as he himself said, in the midst of "an outcast and despised people," could believe that that people "had long drunk of the cup of as great liberties as any people we can hear of under heaven, possessed of freedom from wolfish priests, from civil war, from Presbyterian tyrants, and from our godly Christian magistrates." But, he was obliged to add, "These freedoms have made men wanton and forgetful, and it may be that though we enjoy liberties of soul and body it is license we desire ... I have been charged with folly for that freedom and liberty which I have always stood for ... but blessed be God, who faileth not, and blessed be his name for his wonderful providences, by which alone this town and colony and that great cause of truth and freedom of conscience hath been upheld this day." One may not wonder that in 1669, when sixty-six years of age, after thirty years of wrestling with a stubborn and obdurate people, he could speak of his "worne and withered brain."

It has been necessary to say something about each of these five men in order to show the diverse and often antagonistic personalities that had a place in Rhode Island during the first fifty years of its history. Leaders they were in their respective homes, and representative of their followers, men and women, the latter strong-minded and tenacious, with definite opinions and the will to enforce them, filled with distrust of a central authority and a deep-seated dislike of any power superior to that of the towns in which they lived. Everywhere in the colony was a lack of cohesion, a want of mutual confidence, an excess of desire for personal liberty, which inevitably led to divisions and disorders. Under such circumstances we are not surprised that the movement towards centralization and a united colony was halting and slow. The centrifugal forces were strong. There was at first no common government, no common political organization, no willingness to accept any one man or set of men to whom civil obedience should be rendered. There was no unity in political ideas and administration, no common church, no prevailing habit of religious thought, no singleness of purpose in the hearts of the people.

The first movement towards consolidation was a part of Coddington's scheme for the erection of the island of Aquidneck in Narragansett Bay as a separate government or colony under his own control. To that end he brought about, in March 1640, the uniting of Newport and Portsmouth under a single authority, with himself as governor. This government drew up a remarkable instrument of agreement, which declared the new state to be a democracy or popular government in which none was to be accounted a delinquent for doctrine. It planned a seal which should bear a sheaf of arrows bound up, with the device "Love conquers all" indented within it. Unfortunately, this loving union of two towns, which was outwardly a voluntary combination of two independent sovereignties but in reality a preliminary step in Coddington's ambitious plan for an island propriety of his own, lasted but seven years, when the inhabitants of Portsmouth in 1647 withdrew to be as "free in their transactions as any other town in the colony."

That which broke up this island combination and checked, for the moment at least, the founding of two colonies within the territory of modern Rhode Island, was the successful effort that Williams made at this juncture to hold all the towns together. It was not Coddington with his private aspirations but Williams with his longing for a more perfect union that started these towns on their way towards their first federal organization. So threatening was becoming the Coddington plan for a separation of island and mainland, to further which a royal charter was sought, but in vain, for Aquidneck in 1642; so serious were the claims of Massachusetts and Plymouth and certain land speculators to parts of the Rhode Island area; and so doubtful was the title to land based solely, as it was, on purchase from the Indians, that in 1643 Williams determined to go to England to obtain a patent from the Long Parliament. He wanted a confirmation of the Indian purchases and a warranty of some sort for a government. Forbidden by the Massachusetts magistrates to sail from Boston, he made his way to the Dutch settlement of New Amsterdam in March of that year, and about four weeks later reached England, where he found the country in the throes of civil war. Having secured his patent, through the influence of Warwick, Vane, and others, who were members of the parliamentary committee on plantations, he threw himself into the fray, fighting not with arms but with the pen, and soon after his arrival wrote the *Bloudy Tenent*, composed in haste and published secretly and anonymously, as his contribution to the controversy then raging between the Presbyterians and the Independents. The strange title is explained in Williams's own phrase, "O! how dimme must needs that eye be, which is *blood shot*, with that *bloody* and cruell *Tenent* of Persecution for cause of *Conscience!*" In issuing this work, which was soon burned in England by the common hangman, Williams exercised a powerful influence upon insurgent thought, which was greatly agitated at the time over such questions as liberty of conscience, the separation of church and state, and the right of the people to elect their governors. This famous work became the handbook of the Independents, Sectarians, and Levelers and in some measure at least sowed the seed for the revolution of 1648 and the victory of the Independent party in England.

Williams returned in September 1644, bearing a safe-conduct from the committee for passage through Massachusetts, which the authorities there did not dare disregard, and was received with enthusiasm by his friends and neighbors of Providence. The patent which he had obtained authorized the union of Providence, Portsmouth, and Newport under the name of the Incorporation of Providence Plantations. It put a stop for the moment to the Coddington plot for an Aquidneck charter and a separate government for that island and gave to the whole colony its first great safeguard against encroachment from without and disintegration from within. As events were to show, the struggle between the island and the mainland for dominance was not yet over, but the mainland, which stood for a united colony, had won its first victory over the island, which stood for an independent Coddington domain. More than that — when in May 1647 the patent was put in force at a gathering of representatives at Portsmouth, there was laid the foundations, broad and deep, for a single colony of Rhode Island — foundations which, both in the matters of government and the passing of laws, constitute the understructure of the State of today. That which was done in the year 1647, a noteworthy year in Rhode Island's history, was a long step towards a centralized control away from the powerful forces making for decentralization and a remarkable advance from loosely organized groups of men to a fairly well systematized federal commonwealth.

But it was even more than that. The acts and orders of 1647, adopted at the sessions of the assembly in May, stand as one of the earliest programs of a government and one of the earliest codes of law made by any body of men in America, and the very first to embody in all its parts the precedents set by the laws and statutes of England. By these laws of 1647 a government was set up which covered executive, legislative, and judicial business and distinguished carefully between the powers of the central government and those of the towns. Henceforth, the sovereign towns became but parts of a larger system, retaining corporate rights, as defined in special charters granted to them, but possessing neither legal nor political supremacy. At the head of the new system were a president, four assistants, a recorder or clerk, a treasurer, and a sergeant, all of whom were nominated by the towns and chosen at the court of election in May. Thus, in practice as well as in principle, the government was to be "democratical"; that is, it was to be conducted by the full and voluntary consent of all or the greater part of the inhabitants of the towns who were landowners, as in these early days all of them were. By the adoption of certain specific checks, which are very extraordinary as conceived three hundred years ago, this government was to be prevented from becoming either arbitrary or dictatorial. These checks, born of Williams's determination that civil government should always be controlled by a civil power which lay in the hands of the people of the colony, were frequent elections, short terms of office, the right of towns to initiate legislation, the recall by popular vote of an undesirable law, and the referring of measures before enactment to the people for their approval. These contrivances — initiation, recall, and referendum, all of which have a very modern ring — were retained until the arrival of the charter in 1663. Perhaps the most unusual fact about this impressive body of legislation is that the laws, unlike those of the Puritan colonies, were modeled after the law of England and were founded on the statutes of Parliament, for nearly every one of them, as well as many of a later date, is accompanied by a reference to the English statute book, and all were passed "in the name and power of the free people of this state."

Coddington was not friendly to the patent, as was to be expected, and at this juncture made a determined effort to overthrow it and to destroy, if possible, the unity of the colony by erecting the island into a separate government free to act as it pleased. He entered into negotiations with Massachusetts, Plymouth, and the New England Confederation, and even with the Dutch at New Amsterdam, looking to a possible transference of allegiance, but without result. Finally, he made up his mind to go to England, which he did in October 1649, seven months after the execution of Charles I, in order to petition the Council of State, the executive head of the Commonwealth government, for a special grant or patent of the islands of Aquidneck and Conanicut. He got his commission in March 1651, a document which appointed him for life the governor of the islands, with power to administer the law in the name of the keepers of the liberties of England. This commission made him, to all intents and purposes, a feudal proprietor, a status well suited to a man of his extraction, education, and wealth, who looked with aversion upon the poverty and individualism of Warwick and Providence. But in the final execution of his plan he was unsuccessful. The people of the island rejected his commission, hanged his ally, Captain Partridge, and sent Dr. John Clarke off to England to obtain a recall of his powers. In this mission Clarke, who was accompanied by Williams, was successful. The Coddington *coup d'état* had failed.

On his return from England in 1654 Williams set his hand to the great task of restoring the unity of the colony. Drastic measures were taken, ringleaders of cliques and hostile factions were threatened with trial in England, lesser offenders were condemned to be fined and whipped, and so far was the spirit of the opposition cowed that in 1656 Coddington himself freely submitted to the authority "of his Highness in this colonie as it is now united and that with all my heart." The worst of the danger was over. The united colony had won its victory over the two recalcitrant island towns, Portsmouth and Newport, and the provisions of the patent of 1644 once more became the law of the whole land. Williams never rose to higher levels as a loyal public servant than he did during these two critical years. When peace councils failed he showed, and unexpectedly, the firm hand of the master; and, supported as he was by the authority of Cromwell and the Protectorate and by a majority of the people at large, he was able to swing all the towns into line and to hold the colony together at a time when failure might have meant the extinction of the common government altogether. It is not too much to say that to Williams more than to any other man, not only as founder but as organizer and leader, Rhode Island owes her being.

But an even greater crisis was still to come. Though Coddington was no longer a menace and peace in a large measure had come within the colony, the dangers from without were very real and very threatening. The commissioners of the New England Confederation were unceasing in their efforts to retard the progress of the colony, not only by encouraging encroachments on its lands but also by injuring its economic prosperity. They threatened to cut off its trade, to control the prices of its commodities, and, by refusing to deal with its people except on their own terms, to reduce it to bankruptcy. The situation was rendered the more serious by the news of the restoration of the monarchy in England in 1660. The restoration of the king, Charles II, rendered exceedingly doubtful the validity of the patent of 1644, not only because it was issued by Parliament and not by the king, but also because it had furnished the opportunity for Rhode Island to enforce principles of government that were in many important particulars analogous to those of the Commonwealth and the Protectorate, which England had just discarded. Would the king set aside his royal scruples and give the colony the legal protection that it so imperatively needed, or would he and his advisers refuse the charter of incorporation that alone would give it royal protection and permanence? The great work of building the colony was only half completed. To peace within must be added security from without. Williams had been the man who in storm and stress had kept the towns of the colony together, but he was not to be the one who was to win the greatest of all the colony's blessings – the royal charter of incorporation, without which his efforts would, in all probability, have come to naught and the power of the colony to repel its aggressive neighbors irreparably impaired. The man who did this was Dr. John Clarke.

There is no opportunity here to discuss the negotiations that ended happily in the issue of the charter of 1663, important and instructive as those negotiations are. The document in outward form and legal phraseology is an instrument of the usual type of an incorporated trading company's charter but, like that of the neighboring colony of Connecticut granted the preceding year, it differs from the customary run of such charters in one very noteworthy particular. Instead of creating something new, it merely confirmed a government that was already a going concern and had been such for a long time. That is, it ratified all that had been done under the patent of 1644 and it embodied in its text, with some slight variations, the forms and methods of administration that had been in operation since the passage of the laws of 1647 and following years. Thus, after 1663 the constitution of Rhode Island did not differ materially from what it had been before the charter was granted. But in giving confirmation to what Rhode Island had thus far accomplished it did vastly more than simply set the seal of the king's approval upon the right of these people to occupy a portion of the royal domain in America. It guaranteed, and for the first time and permanently, the legal existence of this outcast among the New England settlements and placed it, as a lawfully chartered political organization, upon the same footing as its proud neighbors, Massachusetts and Connecticut, that had hitherto claimed preëminence and superiority. It did even more. It raised Rhode Island to a legal level higher than that of the two other important members of the New England Confederation, Plymouth and New Haven, which had never been able to obtain royal charters and were in consequence soon to be swallowed up by their associates in the Confederation – Plymouth by Massachusetts in 1691 and New Haven by Connecticut in 1665. It is difficult not to believe that had Dr. John Clarke failed in his mission Rhode Island would have gone the way of the others and eventually have been divided between the two surviving Puritan colonies, which would doubtless have had a glorious encounter, quarreling over the remains.

But now Rhode Island had won her full right to exist, whether the New England Confederation liked it or not. The latter cannot have viewed with equanimity this royal recognition of a colony that its members had formerly deemed beyond the pale of their approval and had refused to admit to their councils. But however much they may have disliked the king's recognition of this plague spot of erroneous political notions, they must have been far more disquieted by the king's confirmation of the colony's highly prized religious ideas, to conserve which Rhode Island was founded. Imbedded in the charter is a memorable phrase establishing the right of that colony to perpetuate the very liberty of conscience to which the Puritans were so unalterably opposed. "That no person within the colonie [so reads the charter] at any time hereafter, shall be anywise molested, punished, disquieted, or called in question, for any difference in opinions in matters of religion . . . but may from tyme to tyme, and at all tymes hereafter, freelye and fullye have and enjoye his and their owne judgements and consciences, in matters of religious concernments . . . not using this libertie to lycentiousnesse and profanenesse, nor to the civil injurye or outward disturbance of others." No one can doubt that Roger Williams penned these words in his instructions to Clarke, for the latter had already reproduced them in all essentials in his petitions to the king; nor can we fail to remark that this was an extraordinary clause to receive the royal imprimatur only three years after the fall of Cromwell and the Protectorate, only a year after the passage of the Act of Uniformity in 1662, and at a time when the Cavalier Parliament was performing its dual rôle of persecuting the Nonconformists in England and of reëstablishing the Anglican church there. Sundry writers have raised the constitutional question whether in the face of this act of uniformity the king had a legal right to commit such a breach, as this was, of the unity and uniformity of a religious faith and discipline that by law had just been established in England. The answer probably lies in the fact that the law of 1662, by its own terms, was not intended to include the colonies but was to apply to England only.

Thus was Rhode Island founded, thus was she maintained, and thus was she enabled to rise as an independent and self-respecting colony and State out of what seems to have been very unpromising conditions. There were many troubles yet to come, prolonged controversies over her boundaries, a bitter and harrowing series of litigations pursued by William Harris for the possession of about a third of the colony's landed area, and moral conflicts with other colonies at critical periods of colonial and national history. None of these, however, ended disastrously. Yet despite this fact and despite the possession of the charter and the successful integration of her territory, Rhode Island would have remained a relatively inconspicuous colony had it not been for the commercial greatness of Newport. During the colonial period Newport was synonymous with Rhode Island, for the back country was neglected save as it furnished surplus products for Newport's ships. In time that island seaport became the third largest center of trade in the entire colonial area. Nevertheless, even with the wealth and sea-borne traffic of Newport, the social charm of old Narragansett, and the activities of the people about the bay in privateering, war, and the slave trade, Rhode Island continued to bear unmistakably the marks of her origin. Never highly centralized, always afraid of executive power, and distrustful of delegated authority, she preserved an attitude of sensitiveness and suspicion and an attachment to local law and local independence that often, in the years to come, determined the relations of the towns to the colony and of the colony to the outside world.

Rhode Island suffered the fate of other Utopias. Soul liberty, though at no time seriously impaired, suffered a disastrous blow with the disfranchising of the Roman Catholics in 1729 and the disbarment of Jews from holding public office, when Williams's doctrine that no man should be excluded from civil rights because of his religious opinions was cast aside and a qualification imposed based on what a man believed in matters of faith. The right of all men to have a part in government, which seems inherent in Williams's interpretation of the "consent of the people," was abrogated from the beginning by the definition of a freeman as a landowner and not as an individual apart from his property; and this qualification was retained long after all but one of the States of the Union had rid themselves of the incubus. Williams's longing for harmony, his cultivation of the spirit of humility, and his willingness to make sacrifices for the common good were menaced by the presence in the colony and State of that individual and offish attitude which found expression in many later acts of noncoöperation with the other colonists and with the Federal Union. The law of 1652 against Negro slavery, of which Gorton was probably the author, proved to be little more than a statement of good intentions, for it was never enforced and was a mere irony in the eighteenth century, when Rhode Island had no less than four thousand Negroes, largely in the towns along Narragansett Bay, with Newport the center of the slave trade. One of the ablest governors that Rhode Island ever had, Stephen Hopkins, was defeated in an exciting town-versus-country political conflict in 1762, largely because of the zeal he showed for a union of the colonies and sympathy with the

larger interests of the British world. The march towards democracy and the progressive development of the social order,
which Williams saw as in a vision, was checked by the rise of a
monopolistic landowning minority that brought upon the State
the Dorr rebellion of 1842. Of this rebellion Williams would
certainly have approved, for he believed that as bodies of
people had fundamentally in themselves the root of power to
set up what governors they agreed on, so they had the right to
tear down these governors if they later proved arbitrary or
perverse. It is a rather remarkable fact that the only New
England State which has never been represented in the President's cabinet is the State of Rhode Island and Providence
Plantations.

Roger Williams was a visionary with great confidence in
human liberty and a stock of ideas that are often modern in
their implications, far more so than those of Winthrop, Endecott, or Davenport, or any of the other Puritan leaders in
Massachusetts or New Haven. On the other hand, he was not
a statesman, for despite his good work for the colony in the
years from 1654 to 1656 he was not well versed in matters of
law or practical government or in the business of setting up a
central organization with an efficient and commanding executive authority. His insistence on freedom in church and state
and the results that followed therefrom have given rise to
the epigram, which contains more than a modicum of truth,
that in the beginning Massachusetts had law but not liberty
and Rhode Island liberty but not law. The license that accompanied the attempts of Williams to apply his ideas of conscience and conduct, the vagueness of the early land deeds,
and the looseness of the early political structure made for
nearly thirty years of dissension, which for a time destroyed
the harmony of the settlements and delayed unity and peace.

Few if any States in our history have suffered more than

has Rhode Island from the conflict between ideals and realities or have had to struggle more earnestly to establish and maintain principles of government and conduct, which were far in advance of their age. Tendencies towards separatism, noninterference, and excessive cautiousness and circumspection were to neutralize there, as they have done elsewhere, some of the higher ethical and political standards. Rhode Island's history demonstrates the truth of the statement that communities founded on utopian schemes, fashioned with too little regard for the complexities and varieties of real society or for the collective experiences of mankind, have either been short-lived, or, in the course of their development, have had to modify in considerable measure their original purposes and ideas.

V

CONNECTICUT: AN ISOLATED PURITAN
AGRICULTURAL COMMUNITY OF STEADY
HABITS

C ONNECTICUT is in origin a Puritan State, of the same
flesh and blood as Massachusetts, and represents in her
beginnings, even better than her neighbor, the Puritan ideal
of a Heavenly City of God, protected from the outside world
by the hedge which Cotton Mather wished to erect against the
wild beasts of the ungodly to safeguard God's people from
contamination and defilement. She stood among the other colonies in a class by herself – a small, inconspicuous agricultural
community, admirably contrived for the purpose of keeping
alive the habits and traditions of her founders, with few of the
political and commercial contacts that opened for Massachusetts the doors for the admittance of wealth and carnal ideas.
With no Anglican church in her midst, such as Boston had after the coming of Andros, with scarcely any incomers of foreign stock, and with a minimum of relations with the mother
country, Connecticut in colonial times was able to keep herself
free from the taint of theological controversy, however much
her people may have exhibited in their personal conduct and
relations the very human qualities that our ancestors were wont
to ascribe to original sin and the wiles of the evil one. The
position, environment, and connections were peculiarly favorable to the retention of Puritan conformity, unchanged in all
essential particulars. In consequence, Connecticut became, in
a remarkable degree, the home of a simple, unaffected Puritan life, and carried aloft the torch of Puritanism even after
Massachusetts had begun to descend the slippery path towards
Unitarianism and heterodoxy. She remained persistently or-

thodox for many years after the Revolution, retaining a single church organization, dominated by a single habit of political and religious thought, and influenced, at least officially, by a consistently uniform religious purpose. It is not surprising that she established a habit of conservative policy and practice which has lasted until the present day. Connecticut's history is the story of the most conventionally Puritan of all the Puritan communities.

This remarkable colony was settled in the years from 1634 to 1636 by emigrants from the Massachusetts towns of Dorchester, Newtown, and Watertown. The movement culminated in the famous journey of the Rev. Thomas Hooker with the members of his church of Newtown – the modern Cambridge – along the Indian path westward towards the Connecticut River, to a final resting place at what today is the site of the city of Hartford. These courageous pioneers were dissatisfied with the conditions that prevailed in Massachusetts and yielded to the charm of the wide meadows of the Connecticut valley and the opportunities which that valley offered for the establishment of plantations. So fertile a region, fed by a broad navigable stream, where land was to be had for the purchasing and where there was freedom to erect a colony independent of all outside authority, proved an allurement not easy to resist. Pasture and meadow were becoming scarce at the Bay and, to a people whose interests at this time were entirely rural and whose prosperity was dependent on their stocks of cattle, goats, and swine, the confines of the towns were becoming too narrow and circumscribed for them. The people of Newtown had early complained of the dryness and sandiness of the soil and the insufficiency of their grazing quarters and, tiring of tillage, had desired to turn to the raising of cattle as a more profitable and less wearisome pursuit. To the mass of the Puritan people, land was still, as it always had been, a leading object of their ambition and its possession a necessity in an agricultural age.

To the leaders of the movement there were other causes of discontent. Such men as Thomas Hooker, John Haynes, and Roger Ludlow were out of sympathy with Winthrop's management of affairs in Massachusetts and with the limitations of the Bay system, and wished to try experiments in a little world of their own. Hooker and Haynes were the Moses and Aaron of the new wandering of the Israelites; and Ludlow, trained in the law, of a masterful disposition and none too certain a temper, was the directing agent who translated into legal form the common ideas regarding government and administration. Others of lesser prominence were doubtless in accord with these three and eagerly embraced the opportunity to separate from Massachusetts and to find a new field for that exercise of leadership which was practically denied them at home. Many of them found Massachusetts a difficult place to live in because of the differences of opinion that prevailed there and because of the overshadowing importance of the magistrates and clergy with their rigid and inelastic methods of oligarchic control.

Hooker had other and more personal reasons. Friendly as he was with John Cotton—the powerful pastor of the Boston church—he disagreed with him on certain important matters of doctrine, intimately bound up with the Antinomian controversy. Cotton held that faith was built upon Christ, not upon sanctification obtained from preaching, teaching, and good works, and that man first attained assurance of faith of his justification by the witness of the spirit of Christ in a free promise of grace. He declared that faith went before works; that in receiving "the Guift of ffaith wee are meerly passive, that in receiving Christ or the spirit of Christ we be passive also"—"an empty vessell fit to receive Christ and his Righteousness"; and that sanctification was but a "created Guift" and a "secondary witness." He took the ground that sanctification could not be the first evidence of justification; that "a faith made by a word [preaching and teaching] and a work [some outward act] without the witness of the spirit and *before it* was not a faith wrought by God's Almighty Power"; and that "the word without the Almighty power of the spirit was *a dead letter.*" He said that the controversy with Hooker ("if it be indeed [he added] a Controversie and not some mistake, as I would gladly hope it is") was not the opposition "between Grace and Works," but "betweene Grace and the merritt of Works," or, as he elsewhere puts it, "betweene Grace and the debt to works," a subtle distinction. All of this Hooker denied. As in his debate later with Roger Williams over the question of liberty of conscience, so in his argument with Hooker over the question of a covenant of grace, Cotton entered upon an involved presentation of his subject, rather easier, however, to understand than is the case with the polemics of some of the other Puritan divines. His first statement was followed by an answer from Hooker, to which he replied. Hooker replied again and Cotton counter-replied. None of these replies is in existence, as far as I know. We learn of the encounter from Cotton's final summary of the argument, which was sent to England, probably in 1637, on nine small sheets of paper, covered with so fine a writing as to be hardly decipherable. The subject of the disputation shows that in origin the event dates back to the days when Cotton was a Hutchinsonian sympathizer and Hooker with a majority of the Massachusetts clergy were on the other side. These differences of opinion in doctrinal matters, in which Cotton at the time was the more liberal thinker, may well have been accentuated by the fact that Hooker held more progressive ideas than did Cotton regarding the share of the people in the affairs of government – ideas that were not capable of application in a colony where church membership was a qualification for freemanship and where the magistrates were deemed the emissaries of God. Each of these men was an oracle in his own community and, as the historian Hubbard says, nature did not allow two suns to shine at the same time in the same firmament. Cotton Mather adds the equally wise remark that two such great men were likely to be more serviceable apart than together.

The promised land of Connecticut to which these people came was of such a character as to set its stamp indelibly upon the later history of those who dwelt therein. Unlike Massachusetts and Rhode Island, the Connecticut territory was not favorable to concentration either of people or of government. It had a long coast line and four or five great river valleys but no single, commodious harbor where commercial activities could converge and where contacts could be made with the outside world. Hence, during the colonial period Connecticut never developed any single center of mercantile and trading interest to compare with Boston or Newport. Her people became widely scattered as one after another of the seventy towns, in the years before the Revolution, were settled by groups of men and women seeking homes wherever they could find a favorable opportunity. Despite the oneness of her political and ecclesiastical organization and the uniformity of her religious belief, Connecticut always found association and coöperation difficult of attainment, and colony and towns rarely entered into combination for the common benefit of the whole. Therefore, the inhabitants of the towns were more or less isolated, their energies were centered largely upon their own agricultural pursuits, and their lives were in the main peaceful and undisturbed. They were free from the political complications that distracted many of the other colonies and were concerned chiefly with the problems of everyday life that arose among the members of their own households, and with the somewhat contentious and censorious habits of the very human population that was trying to make a living, largely as farmers and husbandmen, out of a land of only moderate agricultural fertility. Connecticut's career in colonial times is neither dramatic nor sensational, it contains no highly articulated series of historical events, and is almost entirely without those colorful incidents – conflicts and disorders – that kept other colonies in a more or less constant state of disturbance. We shall pay very little attention here to the conventional course of Connecticut's story, for the importance of the colony lies rather in the men it created and the ideas and institutions it developed than in the more spectacular happenings that give variety and vivacity to the life of any community.

Connecticut stands alone, in a class by herself, as something unique among the British colonies in the New World – a small, slow-moving agricultural settlement, occupying but a tiny part of the earth's surface, largely isolated from the main currents of English and colonial life, and free to enforce, without obstruction and without restraint, the ideas that were working within the minds of her leaders. She offered a remarkably favorable environment within which to experiment with these ideas. Racially, her territory was occupied almost entirely by men and women of pure English stock. Socially, she had few rich and few poor, few large estates and few small ones, little class feeling and no caste distinctions, however much social differences may have played a part in politics, society, and the ecclesiastical order. Economically, she enjoyed an equable distribution of wealth, acquired mainly from farms and farming even in the river and coast towns, where a limited commerce supplemented the somewhat meager returns that accrued from a tilling of the soil. Religiously, she possessed but one church, one prevailing habit of religious thought, one dominating religious purpose in the hearts of her people, one controlling policy that directed her government towards religious ends and proclaimed her for what she was, a religious Puritan state, set apart from the rest of the world as a home and refuge for the people chosen of God and sanctified to his glory.

In the beginning these people, numbering only a few hundred, settled in three plantations bearing the familiar English names of Hartford, Wethersfield, and Windsor, but so closely were they joined in thought and purpose as to constitute a single Puritan body. In the wilderness, three thousand miles from England and widely separated from their nearest neighbors at Boston, Providence, Saybrook, Springfield, and New Haven, like the Pilgrims at Plymouth they were thrown largely upon their own resources and, unhampered by any formal document emanating from the royal chancery, were free to frame such government as they pleased and to put into practice such principles as seemed to their leaders fundamental to the true organization of the state. To that end in the year 1638 they drew up, through the general court of the colony composed of magistrates and deputies from the towns, a document, issued on January 14, 1639, known as the Fundamental Orders, which has attained a conspicuous place in our colonial history. This document consists of a preamble or covenant of agreement to form a government and eleven orders or laws defining that government in general terms. It was an instrument based on the theory of the social compact, the natural expression of a general will, not of three towns in federation but of the people of all the settlements taken together. It was the creation of an already established government that had been functioning for nearly three years and performing important civil, religious, and military duties, a form of political life that contained within itself the germ of a great idea, the idea of self-government.

The preamble of the Fundamental Orders is a plantation agreement, not differing in principle from similar agreements which were signed by groups of people planning to settle together in Plymouth, Rhode Island, and New Hampshire, as well as elsewhere in Connecticut. It was the counterpart of the church agreement, which was the outward and visible sign of a covenant to constitute a church by entering into a combination with God, and it took the form of a mutual understanding and voluntary accord borrowed from the church and applied to the state. The eleven orders that follow the preamble are a body of statute law, not the provisions of a constitution properly so called, and from time to time as need arose they were added to by the assembly itself, which passed laws to modify or alter its previous enactments. The Connecticut document is exceptional in one important particular. It differs from similar documents of Plymouth, Rhode Island, and New Haven in that it takes the form of a concise, well-systematized frame of government, cast in a constitutional mold, and covering briefly and in simple, clear-cut language the essential features of a system such as Hooker wanted and Ludlow was able to draw up. Just as the leading features of the Rhode Island laws of 1647 and of the government that followed were reproduced in the charter of 1663, so the essential features of the Fundamental Orders of Connecticut and of the changes that were made in the ensuing twenty years were embodied in that colony's charter of 1662. And just as the underlying principles of the Rhode Island charter find expression in the present constitution, adopted in 1842, so the principles of the Connecticut charter can be seen underlying the existing Connecticut constitution of 1818.

Thomas Hooker, who had watched the lawmaking going on in Massachusetts and Plymouth and was more in sympathy with the political ideas of Roger Williams than he was with those of John Winthrop, had frankly told the latter that he could not live under the oligarchic system of the Bay colony. It is not impossible that he had derived his political ideas from Roger Williams, whom he knew well and had visited in Rhode Island, just as Williams may have derived some of his ideas from Plymouth, where he had lived for two years. These ideas of Hooker and Williams seem to have been based on the conviction that if only the people could control government, if only sovereignty could be lodged with all the members of a community and be exercised by them, then these same people would in time work out a true commonwealth, a political order based on principles of justice. It is a remarkable fact that in none of his printed works does Hooker give us a hint of what he thought on political matters and that our sole sources of information should be a deciphered outline of a sermon taken down in shorthand and some expressions of opinion in a letter or two. It is doubtful if these ideas were as logically carried out in Connecticut as were those of Roger Williams in Rhode Island, where possession of land seems to have been required but no oath of fidelity excluding Jews, Quakers, and atheists, such as was the case in Connecticut. Evidently Connecticut had no idea of following Williams to the extent of admitting to a share in government anybody or everybody without regard to their religious opinions. As the years went on and new generations followed the old, restrictions of a property sort crept in until those sharing in government, notably in the colony and to a lesser extent in the towns, were very far from coincident with the adult male population as a whole. It is an interesting and suggestive fact that Connecticut and Rhode Island were the last of the original thirteen colonies to throw off a money or property qualification upon the right to vote, thus showing that states utopian in their origin sometimes display in their development extraordinary contradictions.

But Connecticut was not only a homogeneous and consistent Puritan colony in which a considerable measure of popular management was fundamental to her existence, but she was also, and perhaps most strikingly of all, a colony exercising all the rights of self-government, largely independent of the royal prerogative and the king's executive officials in England. In the midst of the British colonial world, while other colonies were undergoing alterations in their political status and, during the eighteenth century, were one by one changing into royal dependencies, this Puritan colony, so small as to be hardly visible from across the water, was enjoying in all parts of its governmental system an approximately complete control of its own affairs. Though a British colony and owing the king loyalty and obedience, it was in fact conducting itself as a petty autonomous state, choosing its own governor, magistrates, and assembly, appointing practically all its own officials, making its own laws, which were valid as long as they did not run counter to the laws of England, exercising its own justice, and raising its own revenue, no part of which, except the royal customs dues, was ever collected by or for the crown. It honestly and obediently acknowledged its allegiance to the king of England, issuing writs in his name and establishing the office of king's and queen's attorney for "impleading in the law all criminal offenders." It required that its governors take the oath to enforce the acts of trade and navigation, sent answers to the queries of the Board of Trade and copies of its laws whenever asked for, admitted a royal customs official into its chief port, and accepted royally appointed commissioners for the determining of its boundaries. In general, it was, by its own declaration made in 1723, "as subject as any other colony to his Majesties commands and to the laws provided for them" and "as solemnly engaged in our fidelity to his Majesty and have as true and sincere allegiance to King George as any of his subjects within his dominions." This attitude to the mother state was due to its being governed by shrewd and tactful men, who saw no objection to obeying the royal commands as long as doing so did not seriously affect the colony's unity and independence. At the same time it was able over and over again, when it was necessary to make good its assertion that the king and his appointees had no right to interfere in its affairs, to interpose its charter between itself and the crown; and it always tried to prevent, though at times unsuccessfully, certain of its people, who were aggrieved for one reason or another, from appealing to England for justice and a reversal of the decisions of its courts. Connecticut during her entire colonial career was largely unknown in England, and it was the object of her leaders to see that she remained so.

That she was able to carry on in her own way in the face of the growing movement towards centralization and empire in the British world of which she was a part, lies partly in the fact of the colony's isolation, partly in her predominantly agricultural character, and partly in the cautious and watchful policy of the Connecticut fathers who labored to prevent this Puritan commonwealth from coming more often than possible to the attention of the British authorities. Connecticut was not, as I think can be justly asserted, "a dutiful colony, attentive to the interest and welfare of the mother country," and the reason is not difficult to find. The object of Connecticut's existence was to serve God and not the king, and she served the king only so far as that service did not imperil the integrity of church and state, whereby alone God's will was to be obeyed. It was the aim of the Connecticut fathers to maintain throughout the colony essential uniformity in political ideas and religious doctrine and discipline; and this policy could not obtain if Connecticut were to become a royal colony, dependent on the crown for her chief officials and they upon the same authority for their instructions as to how the government was to be carried on. No student of Connecticut's history can be surprised for a moment at the determined resistance the colony made, over a period of seventy years, to obstruct the various efforts originating in England and having as their object the breaking down of the colony's independence. But success was not always due to the persuasive tongues and strategic methods of the colony's governors in America or of its agents in England, for certain conditions overseas favored the colonists. Parliament itself was unwilling to strengthen the king's hand by increasing in America the prerogative that it was gradually reducing to a nullity at home, and the landed gentry of England who formed a majority in the House of Lords and the House of Commons were equally unwilling to destroy such a valuable franchise as Connecticut had in her charter. Thus Connecticut and Rhode Island continued to the end the most independent and detached of all the colonies, as far as English interference was concerned, and were the only ones in America possessing and exercising complete self-government.

The bases of Connecticut's political and religious life were the groups of her people gathered into towns and plantations, sometimes embracing a single church and sometimes a number of churches, but all bound together for the worship of God and the management of their secular affairs. These groups constituted, when taken altogether, a loose congeries of towns and churches, each of which, within its own borders, was to all intents and purposes a self-sustaining unit, a petty town and church state, organized for the mutual welfare of its members. The powers it possessed and the privileges it exercised were carefully and liberally defined by the general assembly of the colony and were never exceeded by the towns or encroached upon by the court, so that each town and church was practically independent, itself self-governing within the larger self-governing state. Thus Connecticut was made up of a collection of self-contained rural communities, each of which, under its minister, justice of the peace, and locally elected officials, conducted its business, both prudential and religious, in accordance with the general principles that governed the whole. These little communities were in the main cut off from much contact with the outside world, knew little of their neighbors, less of the other colonies, and almost nothing of what was going on in England or on the Continent. Such a situation tended to create a spirit of individualism — but not of separatism or jealousy as in Rhode Island — a feeling of local self-sufficiency among its towns and churches, and everywhere a highly charged instinct of self-government, which at times was carried to excess in the exercise by small groups and minorities of the right of self-determination and the privilege of expressing their own opinions.

These towns always recognized their subordination to the general assembly of the colony and often said so. The assembly gave them their right to exist and sometimes overruled their decisions, particularly in the matter of land claims and boundaries, and appointed its committees to investigate and report whenever questions arose that the people could not settle for themselves or that were of such a complicated character as to require the interposition of an outside authority. This was not a matter of common occurrence, for the leaders of the colony wanted every town to stand on its own feet and to behave itself as a dutiful town ought to do. Their attitude was distinctly paternalistic, chiding, reproving, remonstrating, but not intervening unless local controversy had proceeded so far and had become so acrimonious as to render intervention necessary. Their tone was rather recommendatory than severe, but they "ordered" often enough to show that they felt quite sure of their right to do so. Individuals and towns engaged in seemingly interminable disputes over boundaries, grants of lands, Indian titles, and such church affairs as the location of a meeting-house or the calling of a minister, and occasionally they came to the general assembly with their troubles, which at times the assembly refused to be bothered with, or, if the two houses could not agree, got rid of as beyond its power to determine. The towns evidenced their respect for the higher authority by addressing magistrates and deputies as "Honored Fathers," "Fathers of the Commonwealth," and even "Their Worships." On a certain occasion one town began a petition with these words, "Whereas you are by God and his people constituted a court of justice," and another addressed its petition "To our Fathers from whom we hope for relefe and defence against all those that would rong us." These phrases are not without significance. Connecticut kept a watchful but not a jealous eye upon the activities of the towns, while these inferior municipalities accepted without question and without concern their subordination to the central authority, which in a limited way was the representative of the people as a whole.

This loosely knit grouping of towns and churches, which made up the colony of Connecticut, however advantageous it might have been to the formation of character and the development of self-respect, was not conducive to the rapid growth and prosperity of the colony. The towns were not much given to teamwork or to mutual coöperation in matters looking to the general welfare. Each lived for itself and labored to promote its own concerns. The executive branch of the government had no power to plan and carry out any program of general improvement, and the general court or assembly rarely busied itself with legislation of this kind. Many matters that are today provided for by the State were then left to be looked after by the towns as a part of their daily routine. One receives the impression that it took a long time to get things done in Connecticut in colonial days, and that such important business as the care of the poor and the destitute, the criminal and the insane, the control of education, and the making of roads, providing of bridges, draining of lands, clearing of rivers, and the doing of other work that related to communication and transportation was either left to local initiative or postponed, neglected, and sometimes ignored altogether.

The trouble was due partly to an attitude of intense conservatism and caution, partly to a lack of interest in the affairs of this life as compared with those of the life to come, and partly to the pressing need of drastic economy. Connecticut was a colony in which laissez faire was the guiding maxim of public conduct, in which the duration of man's existence on earth was but a time of preparation for the better life to come, and in which counting the cost was deeply ingrained in the minds of the people. There was not enough foreign trade to bring in the necessary supply of hard money, and, except for the copper at Newgate and the iron in the Salisbury hills, Connecticut had no mineral resources of her own. Salaries were paid in anything that was usable, and rates and taxes were met in the products of the earth, chiefly wheat and other grains. The lack of available skill, labor, and capital made manufacturing and commercial enterprise on a large scale impossible, and as late as 1818 there were no manufacturing centers in Connecticut, the leading towns being still rural in character, combining agriculture with a small amount of commerce and shipbuilding. There were no banks, no modern methods of credit, and no way of massing small stocks so as to make available for industry the widely scattered savings of a hundred and fifty thousand or more people who occupied the seventy towns that made up the colony on the eve of the Revolution. Therefore, industry and frugality were the golden rules of the Connecticut farmer, and abatement of taxes coupled with the maintenance of the credit of the colony was the desire and aim of every general assembly. These ends were not, however, often obtained, and it was only after 1756 that successful efforts were made to stabilize the currency and to keep the accounts of the government in lawful money instead of depreciated paper. It is an interesting fact that during the years from 1755 to 1764 money was plentiful in the colony, the government was nearly out of debt, and the taxes, though heavy, were borne without complaint; and it is an even more interesting and somewhat surprising fact that, owing to the parliamentary reimbursements for the colony's expenditures during the Seven Years' War, Connecticut was able from 1765 to 1770 to dispense with all colony taxes whatever. The parliamentary fund, deposited in the Bank of England, was drawn upon when the colony needed money for its current administrative expenses. With characteristic reticence and, it may be added, adroitness, Connecticut was careful that Parliament and the ministry should be largely ignorant of the true state of her financial affairs.

That the colony attained to this highly satisfactory financial position was due rather to the munificence of the mother country than to any efforts of its own to increase its wealth through the industry of its people. The agricultural methods of the Connecticut farmer were primitive and, except as far as they satisfied hunger, unremunerative; and they continued to be primitive and unremunerative as long as land within the colony could be obtained on relatively cheap and easy terms. Before the Revolution, Connecticut's population had not begun to press seriously against the means of subsistence, and the competition of lands outside the colony had not compelled the Connecticut farmer to improve conditions at home. He knew little of better farming methods than those which he employed and was strongly opposed to—and continued to be

opposed to until well on in the nineteenth century – anything
that departed from the old familiar way of doing things. No
foreign devices were introduced during this period; intensive
farming was unknown; and while the advantages of manuring
and grafting were understood, it is not easy to ascertain how
widely they were employed. Then, as now, the farmer suffered from "blastings, mildews, caterpillars, worms, tares,
floods and droughts" and had a well-grounded fear of the bad
effects of barberry bushes on wheat. Farming was on a small
scale; and the average husbandman, having harvested a crop
sufficient for his own needs, made little effort to create a surplus for the purpose of seeking a market either at home or
abroad. There were enterprising men living in the river and
coast towns who freighted vessels with live stock, grain, garden produce, horses, boards and pipe staves, and a small
amount of tar, cider, flax, and hemp, and sent them to New
York or Boston in exchange for manufactured goods, to Ma-
deira for wine, and to the West Indies for sugar, molasses, and
rum; and there were occasional towns with a marketable
staple, such as Wethersfield, which sold its onions for tea,
coffee, sugar, or cash. But these instances are exceptional. The
average Connecticut farmer was afraid of a surplus, for he did
not know what to do with it. Roads were few and often im-
passable, and transportation by oxen and mules was a slow and
exhausting ordeal. Travel was easiest by water, but the rivers,
particularly the Connecticut, were rendered dangerous by
freshets, mud banks, sand bars, and shifting channels, and
were navigable only for vessels of light draft. The coast towns
were always hampered by silt blocking the harbors. The farmer who lived away from the water highways was necessarily
isolated and remote. He saw very little hard money – Spanish
dollars, moidores, and johannes – and was very careful in
spending what he had. He was compelled to rely almost entirely on his own local means of subsistence.

The very isolation of the colony from the world outside and the isolation of the towns from each other made for self-reliance, but it also made for provincialism and an amazing ignorance of what was happening in the other colonies and in the countries beyond the seas. Connecticut was little touched by events outside her own boundaries and was little affected by the laws, customs, practices, and principles that were in vogue elsewhere. She stands as the only colony that did not follow English practice in the proceedings of her legislature or that did not admit into her legal code any considerable amount of English common and statute law. That there was a measure of the common law of England imbedded in the laws and practices of the colony can hardly be doubted, but in most cases the lawmakers went their own way, adhering closely to the law of the Old Testament and to their own ingrained sense of justice. When doubt arose, Connecticut limited herself to "some plain and clear rule of the Word of God" or, as elsewhere expressed, to the administration of justice "according to the Law of God and humane policy" or "according to our lawes and the rule of righteousness." Despite this appeal to righteousness and humane policy, the Connecticut codes contained much that was harsh and arbitrary and liable to abuse. Francis Fane, the standing counsel to the Board of Trade, who commented on the Connecticut laws passed up to 1721, found many that allowed the civil and judicial authorities far too much discretion for the safety and welfare of the people and gave too frequent opportunities for injustice and even oppression. He found some of the laws vague and unreasonable and was not a little puzzled by the extraordinary character of such as imposed capital punishment according to the Mosaic code. Some he considered distinct infringements on personal liberty and others inferior to the corresponding English law because they failed to contain qualifications and safeguards that were deemed necessary in order to protect individual rights. After 1750 the colony conformed more and more to the rules of the English common law, but there can be little doubt that such legal particularism, such deliberate renunciation of the legal experiences of the mother country, were injurious to the legal history of the colony.

The government of Connecticut was never a democracy, in any commonly understood sense of the word. It was popular in so far as elections were held at which the "freemen" or a portion of them cast votes, upon the counting of which certain officials were declared elected and by virtue of which governors, magistrates, and deputies exercised their functions. But under cover of what, to all seeming, was a popular form, there prevailed a system that was aristocratic, paternalistic, and to some extent clerical or at all events religious. Politics were controlled by a very few men, chiefly by a coterie of individuals from the leading towns and families, and they continued to be so controlled until well on in the nineteenth century, even after the religious coloring of the colony had faded away and the new constitution had supplanted the old charter, so deeply rooted was the habit of accepting dictation in the popular mind and so fixed was the idea that government should be in the hands not of the "people" but of those who represented property, orthodoxy, and family inheritance. The tenure of the governor was practically for life, and during the eighteenth century but two in that office when presented for reëlection were ever defeated. Death, senility, or other unavoidable causes brought careers to an end, but only in two cases was popular disapproval the determining factor.

These Connecticut leaders did not represent the "people" and were not intended to do so, for there were no such things as short terms, rotation in office, or giving every man a chance. They represented the elect of the colony, those who were most worthy in the sight of God and man to govern by virtue of their orthodoxy, family, wealth, talents, education, and political experience. The voters exercised very little independence of choice in the naming of candidates; their chief business was to vote, and as a rule, to vote to continue in office those who were already there. Their attitude was one of acquiescence rather than of active determination. There were no silver-tongued orators to arouse discontent in an appeal for votes, no parties claiming the allegiance of followers and promising in case of success "to turn the rascals out"; no plum trees, no bribery, no graft. The effort to keep men in power was less for party purposes than to preserve intact the principles and standards of a Puritan ideal and to preserve unaltered an attitude of conservatism and steady habits. Adherence to the original purpose for which the colony was founded had become so inwrought as to take the form of a tenet of faith. So strong was the influence of religious conviction in the life of the colony and so masterful the opposition to new and unfamiliar social and intellectual ideas, that change and improvement were as rare in legislative halls as they were in the fields that the farmers cultivated. The duty of those who took part in the elections was to put the right kind of men in office, and the duty of those chosen to office was to maintain government and not to change it. The Connecticut leaders fought to preserve the charter as the palladium of their liberties, not only to retain their political independence of Great Britain but also to make impossible any tampering with a system of government that God had stamped with the seal of his approval. They wanted rule by a democracy as little as they wanted rule by a royal governor.

The government of the colony was monopolized by the standing order, representative of those two most conservative influences in the life of any community, heredity and orthodoxy, the twin pillars of the Puritan system. Sectarian opposition was confined largely to the southern and southwestern parts of the colony and did not attain in colonial times sufficient unity or momentum to affect the dominance of Puritan control. Political opposition hardly existed, for commerce and manufacture had not yet begun—and were not to begin for a hundred years—to play their great rôles as promoters of new ideas along what would have seemed to the men of the colonial period radical and, therefore, dangerous lines. It was no accident that after 1763 the center of opposition to British policy lay east of the Connecticut River in Windham County. There originated the local activities against the Stamp Act; there sprang into being the Sons of Liberty; there found expression some of the most vigorous utterances in support of the nonconsumption and nonimportation measures; and there lived that fine old Puritan war governor and his son-in-law, the signer of the Declaration of Independence, two of the most typical representatives of the standing order of their day, Jonathan Trumbull and William Williams.

The form that the Connecticut government took was the natural expression of those particular Puritan ideals and principles that had taken root in the Connecticut colony. The deputies from the towns in general assembly controlled affairs and there was no centralized leadership either in church or state. The governor was always an eminently respectable man, of unimpeachable integrity and uprightness, who was invariably chosen from among the oldest and most distinguished families, generally resident in one of the leading towns. He was honored and trusted by the old and gazed upon with awe by the young, for he represented the best that the colony could furnish and was the embodiment of all that gave the standing order its divinely invested authority. No ungodly man or one of a dissenting faith could possibly have been chosen by that small body of "freemen" in whose hands lay the casting of votes. They even turned down the affable and thoroughly orthodox Roger Wolcott because they thought he had not done his duty in the Spanish ship case; and they refused to reëlect the conservative and conscientious Thomas Fitch because he stood by his oath to the crown in the Stamp Act troubles and refused to break his bond with Great Britain. To be a governor in Connecticut required that one not only possess all the Puritan virtues but also should stand for the voter's idea of devotion to duty and loyalty to the commonwealth.

The governor, though often personally influential, as the king of England is today, virtually had no power. He had no right of veto, no patronage, no influence on legislation, no control of pardons. He never led the members of the assembly or the voters. On the contrary, the members of the assembly controlled him, kept careful watch upon the exercise of such functions as were allowed him and his council, and required that all matters of importance be submitted to themselves for deliberation and approval. In the earlier days they paid him a miserly salary, but during the boom times of the sixties they increased the amount to £150 a year, a not inconsiderable sum for those days. It was never possible for the governor independently of his council to have any policy of his own or to do anything more than carry out the dictates of those whose mouthpiece he was. In the history of the colony no man in the governor's chair, unless we except Thomas Fitch, who only tried to do what he thought was right in a difficult situation, ever broke the traditions of the order that he represented.

The magistrates, who served in the double capacity of advisory council to the governor and upper house of the assembly, formed a collective group of the same character as the governor, from among whom the latter was always selected. They were dignified, conservative, and in the earlier period inclined to be inquisitive and dictatorial, guardians of Puritan policy and vested interests, and very buttresses of law and order. Being few in number they took a more personal and direct interest in the affairs of the towns and in the seventeenth century might well have been given the title "Nursing Fathers," applied in Massachusetts to the magistrates there during the earlier years in the history of that commonwealth. In their rôle as councilors they exercised a great variety of functions: executive, military, and judicial, making appointments, investigating complaints, issuing orders and offering advice. They carried on correspondence with the royal officials and the colony's agents in England and frequently with the other colonies, notably those of Massachusetts, Rhode Island, and New York. They managed the financial business of the colony and served as a council of war directing military policy. After 1662, for nearly fifty years they sat as a superior court of common pleas under the designation Court of Assistants, until in 1711 a separate superior court was established by act of assembly. They issued proclamations and in general took charge of whatever duties the assembly assigned to them. As long as Connecticut remained a religious colony their efforts were directed to the maintenance of things as they were, and as long as the disintegrating forces within the colony were weak and without cohesion, they had little difficulty in accomplishing their purpose. But, later, when the influence of the French Revolution began to be felt and the animosities against Great Britain began to become fewer, the dislike which they and the other leaders of the standing order had entertained for radicalism in the shape of democracy took the form of an abhorrence for a movement that seemed to them compacted of infidelity, immorality, and political disorder, and they opposed with all their might for half a century longer the changes which the new conditions demanded. The attitude after 1789 was only more intense than it had been before 1776; it did not differ in principle or in kind.

The lower house of assembly may possibly have been somewhat more liberally inclined than the council or upper house, because it represented the towns, a more widely scattered group of constituencies than were the old families and leading communities that controlled the council. But generally speaking it is safe to say that all were cast in the same mold and exhibited about the same habits of mind. The assembly, as a whole, was supreme in the colony and remained supreme even after the adoption of the constitution of 1818, leading President Dwight to say that it could do almost anything except alter the results of an election and the Supreme Court of Errors to confirm the time-honored rule in Connecticut that the assembly could exercise any power not specifically denied by the constitution. During the colonial period it controlled both the executive and the judiciary, and its powers were undefined except by statutes of its own making, for the charter contained no details of government. If both houses agreed, as they frequently did not—and some disagreements, particularly on matters brought before them by petition, lasted for years—the assembly could pass any laws it pleased; it was judge of its own proceedings and guardian of its own privileges. Though its activities embraced judicial as well as legislative business and a certain amount of military supervision and control of military appointments, its range of interest was very limited. It erected townships, granted land that lay outside township bounds, inquired into the validity of Indian claims, permitted the erection of churches and the calling of ministers, levied the colony rate and authorized the expenditure of money for a great variety of purposes, and made provision for bridges, ferries, and sewers for the draining of wet lands. It also took a half-hearted interest in the care of the roads. Even some of these things and many others as well were left to the care of the local authorities. It met the problems that arose year after year, but in all that it accomplished, which in fact was not very much, it presents a picture of men little interested in enlightened or constructive legislation.

The explanation of all this is not very far to seek. Connecticut throughout her entire colonial career, though in constantly decreasing measure, was inclined to neglect the needs and opportunities of the immediate present. She failed of her main purpose as must any body of men fail who try to enforce unchanging rules of life and conduct according to religious formulae and attempt to maintain intact an attitude of religious exclusiveness and isolation from the mutable world about them. But so strong was the hold that the Puritan leaders obtained upon the colony, so general was the sympathy of the inhabitants of the towns with the aims and methods of those in authority, and so honorable, in the main, were the efforts of the government to rule wisely and for the good of all, that Connecticut remained to the end the only British colony constructed according to the Puritan plan of a home for "God's chosen people." The oligarchic system eventually fell, not, as had that of Massachusetts, before the attack of the British crown in an effort to draw it within the fold of the British system, but before the determination of those within the state itself to bring into a better accord with the times a Puritan control that had already outlived its usefulness. Like the walls of Jericho, the defenses of the Puritan City of God crumbled before the blasts of a democracy that was slowly attaining the stature of a man – a democracy that the Puritans of colonial days and those that continued to survive well on into the nineteenth century distrusted as an aberration of the human mind, disapproved of God and his faithful elect.

Another striking characteristic manifests itself in colonial Connecticut. The Puritan fathers and mothers had a high sense of that which has been called the genius of the American republic, personal responsibility, but they did not always realize that such responsibility reaches its perfect form only when working in combination with other responsibilities in community, state, and nation, and that an overdeveloped individualism that sees only its rights and privileges and not its duties and obligations towards man as well as God is neither profitable nor of permanent importance. Too much stress has been laid upon individual liberty as the keystone of human society. In any social group it is always a matter of difficulty to determine where rights end and duties begin and at what point liberty passes into license. The idiosyncracies of individuals and minorities are not always contributory to the common stock of human welfare, and allowance of them is permissible only when the greater issues of the social order are not endangered. Perhaps the most perfect rights are those that presuppose duties as their necessary complements, and the most perfect liberty that which recognizes as essential to its existence obedience to the social law. This more complete conception of personal responsibility and personal liberty was scarcely understood by our Connecticut ancestors, whose sense of obligation went but little beyond the confines of their individual towns and churches. They were trained in the stern discipline of labor and duty and were profoundly convinced of their personal responsibility towards God and the moral law, and this it was, more than anything else, that guided them in their lives of endurance and self-control; but they had no clear notion of the management of men in the mass or of the orderly regulation of human wills by a common spirit enlarging and enriching their daily routine. Such an idea of social relationship never entered into their minds.

Connecticut's claim to distinction in American history rests upon several indisputable facts. In the first place the colony set before the other colonies a remarkable example of a political community entirely self-governing and relatively at peace with itself. Whatever quarrels took place were mostly local and in a state of low visibility when viewed from beyond its borders. In the second place it probably provided, in proportion to its size, more men and the ancestors of men that have played a prominent part in the affairs of the nation than any other colony, not excepting even Massachusetts or Virginia. Thirdly, its colonial leaders created a government that in the principles upon which it was based was amazingly advanced for the day, and put into practice ideas and methods that, with all their limitations, represented something very near the ideas and methods that prevail (theoretically at least) in the United States at the present time. They decided that the source of civil and religious authority should be not kings or proprietors, councils or convocations, but such of the people as were deemed worthy to exercise it; that the actual management of affairs should be entrusted not to royal or ecclesiastical appointees or to those whose object was profit or prominence, but to men competent by inheritance, training, respectability, and spirituality to wield it; and that the ends of government should not be the benefit of party or the politician but the furtherance of the common good as they saw it. Their successors did not realize that society cannot remain politically and spiritually stationary without provoking counter-resistance and even revolution, and that continued control by a propertied and capitalist class, no matter how socially and religiously important it be, is bound in the end to arouse the antagonism, as it did in Rhode Island also, of those excluded from a share in government and from the opportunities that position and wealth confer. These men, it is true, administered the affairs of the colony wisely and piloted the ship of state skillfully through many troubled waters. They were able to establish so firmly their system of government and to create within the colony so widespread a feeling of contentment and satisfaction as to bring about the retention of the charter for thirty-five years after independence was secured and to keep in office the members of the same ruling class until well on towards the middle of the nineteenth century. Until the outbreak of the Civil War, Connecticut was dominated by her Puritan heritage of unprogressiveness, and despite the constitution of 1818, which broke the monopoly of the standing order and broadened the base of popular control, she advanced with hesitating and unwilling steps along the path of material improvement and social welfare. Though deviating of late in some measure from her traditional conservative and reactionary policies in matters of legislation, Connecticut even today bears the marks of her Puritan past.

MARYLAND: A FEUDAL SEIGNORY IN
THE NEW WORLD

Thus far we have concerned ourselves chiefly with settlement in America by men of England who were endeavoring, under the authority of trading-companies charters, to make use of the lands overseas for commercial or religious profit. Those who promoted the Virginia Company of London valued their opportunities not so much for the lands they controlled as for the staples these lands produced and the benefits which the sale of these staples contributed to their own exchequer. Theirs was strictly a commercial purpose. The settlers of New England sought not land but a refuge wherein to put into application certain ideas of ecclesiastical polity and religious discipline that could not be tried out at home, and they looked on the territory they received as a place for the planting of a social and political community that would prove a suitable environment within which to carry out the plans of God regarding his chosen people. Theirs was primarily a religious purpose. Neither of these groups of men was representative of England's historical past or of the traditions and practices that characterized the life of a majority of the English people. Relatively speaking, but few in the England of the sixteenth and seventeenth centuries were commercially minded and still fewer were addicted to Puritan notions to such an extent as to render them dissatisfied with their native country.

There was still a third group of people interested in settlement. England was a kingdom in which the possession of land was still the hallmark of quality and the end and aim of every one who aspired to a position of political importance and social influence. It was a kingdom in which the laws regarding the tenure, transfer, occupation, and incidents of the soil were among the most important that concerned the English convey-ancer and lawyer, whose mind was slow to change and who ad-hered with amazing tenacity to the methods and ideas that had long been established in the field of real property. And this condition remained for many years after the sixteenth century had brought certain marked changes in the relation of the landed proprietor to the estates that he held. Two of these changes may be briefly noticed. The fetters were gradu-ally being loosed that had hitherto bound the land within the grasp of the old feudal obligations, and simpler and less re-strictive tenures were being substituted for those that had pre-vailed in the Middle Ages. The freest tenure of the time was that styled free and common socage, the terms of which were fealty and a fixed rent, and this tenure was fast swallowing up all the other tenures because of its convenience and its ready adaptability to a changing land system, which was demanding an easier and more flexible method of acquiring landed prop-erty. Under all the charters which thus far have been brought to your attention, lands were held in free and common socage as of one or other of the king's manors, a form of tenure the most advantageous that the time could possibly afford. In the second place, the landed proprietors of the day, who were de-pendent for their incomes on the rents of their tenancies and on the agricultural profits of their soil, were suffering from the changes accompanying the transition from an agricultural to a mercantile economy. The sixteenth century had been par-ticularly hard on the landed classes. Tenants could not pay their rents and were leaving the manors for the towns and seaports. Prices were rising and the values of land were fall-ing. New lands were obtained with difficulty at home by drain-ing the marshes and fens, and in Ireland by the escheating of conquered territories to the crown, which in turn parceled them out to those who would settle upon them. Woods and forests were being laboriously turned into arable and sheep pastures, and there were never enough to meet the demand. Feudalism and all that it stood for as an agricultural form of social and economic life was passing away, and incomes and profits were decreasing.

In consequence of these conditions, which prevailed not only in the seventeenth century but throughout our entire colonial period, large numbers of men, generally of the better sort, who wished to maintain themselves at court and elsewhere in a manner suitable to their rank and standing, were making every effort to improve their possessions and increase their resources. Men of prominence, both in office and out, saw in America opportunities of adding to their estates and of acquiring large grants of land wherefrom to recoup their failing fortunes. Hence, side by side with the commercial companies and the groups that were colonizing for religious purposes, there arose another class of those who were to play a very important part in the settlement of America, the great landed proprietors. These men wanted to build up estates in America on the English model and to transfer to the new world the ideas and practices with which they were accustomed in the familiar environment in which they had been born and brought up.

One need not be surprised at the appearance during these early years of many striking instances of the transference to America of the feudal and seignorial practices of old England. It would have been far more extraordinary if such practices had not been transferred. We have paid an undue amount of attention to the religious settlement of the Puritans and to the commercial activities of the members of the Virginia and Bermuda companies, largely because they are both easy to understand and more closely related than are proprietary institutions to modern American ideas. Because we do not think today in terms of an aristocratic order of society, we find it hard to comprehend why in dealing with our colonial history we should need to know anything about rules of feudal law that appear to be nothing but fossils from a bygone age. We have overlooked the fact that the normal English society of the seventeenth century was aristocratic, manorial, and agricultural, and that to large numbers of the English people of that time no other system was conceivable. That English expansion should carry many of these ideas and practices into the New World is but natural, and that the modern historian should have some knowledge of the historical background of feudal institutions is necessary if he is properly to interpret life in the American colonies. To study these institutions is generally considered merely an antiquarian pursuit, a diversion of effort that might better be expended in more profitable undertakings, but the fallacy of this contention lies in the fact that though English seignorial and tenurial practices were destined to wither in the uncongenial atmosphere of the wilderness and the frontier, their appearance and struggle for existence in America had an appreciable effect on the lives of the colonists and on the course of colonial development. Nothing that played a part in shaping the activities of colonial life, no matter how difficult or how remote it may be, can be ignored by the student and writer of colonial history.

In its outward form the landed system of England in the seventeenth century was not greatly changed from what it had been two centuries before. The world of the English gentry and landholding class was based upon the possession of the soil, according to the value and extent of which distinctions and social ratings were determined. Little wonder is it, therefore, that with the breaking down of their landed incomes the landed classes in the seventeenth and eighteenth centuries should have looked to the wide expanses of America for relief. Scores of men of these classes – from peers of high rank, who were often long in titles but short in wealth, through all grades of the nobility and the greater and lesser baronetage, to the more humble knight and squire – sought and obtained grants of land in America. Some of these grants were palatinates and lordships, the extent of which embraced ten or twelve millions of acres; others were merely landed proprieties comprising thousands of acres; some were even of lesser extent, obtained by grants from the crown wherever there was unoccupied land to be given from the St. Lawrence to the Floridas. There are scores of such grants in the seventeenth century to men who saw in the financial value of the quitrent a promising source of income. Even in the eighteenth century the hope still remained strong in many an Englishman's heart of financial profit from land in the New World. In 1717 Sir Robert Montgomery, prompted by a desire for revenue from tenancies and rents, obtained from the Carolina proprietors his grant of Azilia, lying between the Savannah and the Altamaha rivers. In 1722 the Duke of Montague petitioned for the islands of St. Lucia and St. Vincent, and in 1728 for the island of Tobago, wherein to erect manors and seignories. In 1731 the Duke of Chandos set on foot an attempt to obtain the "equivalent lands" that Connecticut ceded to New York, for the purpose of creating there a series of English estates. And as late as 1764 Lord Egmont tried to secure a grant of Prince Edward Island on much the same terms as those which were contained in the earlier proprietary charters. These men knew no other form of landholding than that which prevailed on their own estates at home, where manorial relationships were familiar to all and where quitrents, tenancies, freeholders and copyholders, rent rolls, courts leet and baron, and many of the surviving incidents of the Middle Ages still lingered, as they continued to linger well on into the nineteenth century. When these men thought of lands in America and sought to acquire possession of them, the great majority had in mind first of all the revenues that they might derive from the tenants to whom they would let the lands and the profits and perquisites which they were accustomed to receive from their ownership of the soil. They needed tenants that they might add to the income from their estates, for lands unimproved and unoccupied were of as little value in America as they were in England. These members of the nobility, these lesser barons and knights, to whom the possession of land was the sign and symbol of gentility and social prestige, were as eager as any Western homesteader or American land promoter to obtain grants of land, large or small, that might be added to the acres that made up their estates at home.

One cannot understand the history of proprietary government in the English colonies in America without understanding some of these things. From 1621 to 1640, beginning with the Scottish grant of Nova Scotia to Sir William Alexander and closing with the grant of Maine to Sir Ferdinando Gorges in 1639, we have a series of proprietary patents to lands in America and the West Indies that are indicative of the desire which was influencing men in high office in the government of England, in the early years of the seventeenth century, to find estates overseas. Some of these grants were more distinctly feudal than others, for the more feudal the type of grant the more revenue the king would receive from the grantee, and both James and Charles were to no inconsiderable extent dependent upon the royal receipts from their manors, in a day when the king was expected to administer the government in large part from his own resources.

Among these grants one is quite different from the others

and stands among the proprietary patents much as the charters
to Connecticut and Rhode Island stand among those of the
joint-stock type – a document extraordinarily liberal to the
patentee. This was the charter of 1632 to Sir George Calvert,
created Lord Baltimore in the Irish peerage in 1625, which
was issued to his son Cecilius, Sir George having died before it
passed the seals. Its form and character were determined by the
father, not the son, and its peculiarly favorable terms must be
credited to the father's influence with the king rather than to
any desire of the government to favor the proprietors in so
extraordinary a way. Calvert was closely identified with the
activities of the government, and, as secretary of state, a member of the Virginia Company and of the Council for New
England, with extensive land grants in Newfoundland and
Ireland, must have been thoroughly familiar with the different
varieties of patents that were issued and have been well aware
of that particular type which seemed to him most desirable.
There appears to be no doubt that he drew up his own terms,
and that, too, without the knowledge either of the Privy
Council or of the old Virginia Company, the latter of which
though dissolved still hoped to be reinstated. Both of these
bodies entered strong objections when it was too late to do anything about the matter, and all that the Virginia Company was
able to accomplish was to have the grant made north of the
Potomac instead of south of the James, where Calvert had first
wanted it.

The reasons why the Maryland charter was so favorable
to the patentee and, in being so, was to have a far-reaching influence on Maryland history are these. The lands were granted
in free and common socage and not *in capite* or by knight's
service, the former a tenure in which the proprietor paid only
a nominal rent to the king. This rent constituted no burden
upon the proprietor, who was to all intents and purposes en-

tirely free as regards his relations with the crown. On the other hand, Baltimore himself was allowed extraordinary powers. He was given all the rights and privileges of the palatinate of Durham "which any bishop of Durham ever before had enjoyed or ought to have enjoyed." As the bishop of Durham had once had almost regal authority, being a paramount lord in all matters of granting lands to be held of himself and not of the king, it followed that the proprietor in Maryland was free to grant baronies and manors as he pleased, to be held only of himself in as ample a manner as any king in England granted and held them. Furthermore, Baltimore controlled all branches of the government in his colony, executive, judicial, and even legislative in that under the charter he had full right to initiate legislation, and in all other respects exercised the equivalent of that "regal and imperial power which is granted in all things of sovereignty, saving only allegiance to the king's majestie." Thus he owned all the land, received all the profits from it, controlled the government in all its branches, and owed the king only a nominal payment. The king even gave up his peculiarly sovereign right of pardoning criminals, reserving no right of appeal from justice to his own royal person, and relinquished even the right of disallowing laws as long as they were consonant to reason or not contrary to the laws of England. Baltimore became the absolute lord, viceroy, seigneur, and proprietor of the province of Maryland. In his "style," as it is called, that is, the title which he used in issuing commissions, proclamations, writs, and other high official documents, he and his successors continued to employ the form "Absolute Lord and Proprietary of Maryland and Avalon, Lord Baron of Baltimore." Baltimore was a lord of Maryland by divine right, quite as much so indeed as ever was a Stuart the king of England; and he possessed, if we are to interpret the words of his charter literally, even fuller powers in Maryland than the king himself possessed or at least exercised at home. I doubt if even the king at this time could be said to have possessed "full, free, and absolute power to ordain, make and enact laws of what kind soever," and we may doubt if Baltimore or his successors considered the further phrase – "with the advice, assent and approbation of the freemen of the province" – as seriously curtailing their privileges. What these same freemen were eventually to make of their part in colonial legislation is another matter, which does not concern us at this point.

Maryland was settled in 1634 directly from England and was designed at the outset as a place of refuge for English Roman Catholics. It represented the culmination of an effort, which had begun in Elizabeth's day, to find a home overseas for these persecuted religionists in England. But Maryland was never intended by Sir George Calvert or his son Cecilius to be a place of retreat for Roman Catholics only. In the two vessels – the *Ark* and the *Dove* – that sailed from England in October 1633, there were two Jesuit priests, seventeen Roman Catholic gentlemen with their wives, and some two hundred more – handicraftsmen, laborers, servants, and others – a majority of whom were Protestants of the Church of England. These voyagers went by way of the Azores and the West Indies and finally reached Chesapeake Bay in the spring of 1634, landing at the mouth of the Potomac on an island which they called St. Clements. There they took formal possession of the soil "for our Saviour and for our Sovereign Lord the King of England," and at St. Marys, near the southernmost point of the present State of Maryland, they established their government, where they maintained their control for more than half a century.

In their beginnings and in the history of the first twenty-five years of their respective existences no colonies could be

more unlike than Maryland and Massachusetts. Whereas
Massachusetts profited by the condition of affairs in England,
Maryland suffered in corresponding measure. From 1650 to
1660 Massachusetts was on the tidal wave of prosperity, and
the Puritan cause was everywhere in the ascendant. We know
that, had it not been for the financial troubles that came upon
the king of England and his advisers after 1630, for the civil
wars that broke out in 1642, and for the rule of the Puritan
minority from 1649 to 1660, the Puritans would hardly have
been able to identify themselves, their ideas, and their government with New England or to have erected an independent,
sovereign Puritan commonwealth on New England soil. Ex-
actly the reverse was the case with the lord of Maryland and
the proprietary group generally. In the first place the wars in
England prevented many a landed proprietor from taking
part in the colonizing movement, partly by drawing him into
the wars on the side of the king and partly by estopping the
king from issuing grants of lands to those whom he desired
to help and to honor. In the second place, the Puritan victory
placed in an awkward and embarrassing situation the Roman
Catholic Lord Baltimore and the aristocratic Maryland, which
was the only proprietary settlement at that time on the continent of America. The result was that for nearly thirty years,
while Massachusetts was increasing in wealth, power, and territory, Maryland was torn with internal feuds and menaced by
outside dangers. It finally fell into the hands of the Puritans
who had settled at Annapolis in 1651, and Lord Baltimore
lost his government for several years. But in the year 1660,
when Charles II came into his own, the conditions were re-
versed. For Massachusetts the return of the monarchy marked
the beginning of the end for the independent Puritan commonwealth, while, on the other hand, it brought a measure of
security to the Maryland proprietor and made it possible for

him to give full rein to his proprietary privileges. While Massachusetts was fighting her battle with the crown for the right to exist as a sovereign commonwealth, Lord Baltimore was left free to put into operation all his claims to proprietary rule. There is no more suggestive task in the study of our early colonial history than to compare the careers of Massachusetts and Maryland from 1630-1634 to 1689 and to see how it was that neither a religious commonwealth on one side nor a seignorial province on the other was destined to find permanence among our colonial settlements.

Cecilius Calvert, Lord Baltimore, remained in England and governed the province from there as absolute lord and proprietor. His commissions to his administrative officials, in their language and in their assumptions of authority vested in himself alone, surpass anything that ever came forth from the royal chancery itself. To his appointees in the colony he delegated powers in a manner that was more than regal – it was imperial. Even though he might instruct his appointees to exercise these powers with a high regard for tolerance, kindliness, and justice, he took the position that no one existed anywhere, except God and perhaps the king, to dispute his proprietary authority. There can be no doubt of the clemency of the proprietor during this period of Maryland's history, for few appealed to him without relief and few confessed their offenses against him and his government without receiving forgiveness and amnesty. But none could continue to deny or oppose his authority without punishment. He was neither arbitrary, despotic, nor arrogant, but he was absolute lord, even though his prerogative was softened by benevolence.

Cecilius in 1661 appointed as governor in the colony his son Charles – destined to become the proprietor after his father's death in 1675 – and invested him with the entire command of the province. He made him chief governor, commander in chief, lieutenant general, chief captain, and chief admiral, both by sea and land, with all the powers that these titles implied. He appointed the members of the governor's privy council – the "private, secret and continual council" – which the governor was to use as his personal consulting and advisory body, and he enjoined upon his son that he was to add to it only those who were of no lower rank than the lord of a manor. This was a council such as never had been or was to be in all colonial history – a personal council, a feudal council, a council in the proprietor's own hand. It became the bulwark of his authority, and was composed only of those who accepted his full prerogative and would sustain him in the complete exercise of his powers. It tended, as the years went by, to become a family affair, representative only of the proprietor and his interests, in no way standing for the people of the colony, who were strictly commanded to obey its decrees and accept its decisions without murmuring.

This absolute but benevolent proprietor appointed also the chancellor, the chief justice and the secretary, and all the justices of the provincial court, who were to look to him for their authority and to hold their offices only during his pleasure. He invested them with the usual judicial and secretarial powers, to be exercised for the preservation of the peace both of proprietor and province, and he gave them equity jurisdiction and control over matters that concerned his revenue as well as the law and order of the colony. Thus the whole judicial, financial, and administrative business lay ultimately in his hands and was under his complete control. Indeed, so far did he carry this separation of the governing and privileged classes from the rest of the people of the province – whose only privilege under the charter was to approve the laws that the proprietor might make – that he proposed, though there is nothing to show that he ever carried out the proposal, to introduce distinctions of dress, insignia, medals, and the like in order to place the ruling class apart by itself and mark it off from the common herd. That he might emphasize this distinction and increase his personal hold upon the province, he formed a political ring made up largely of his relatives; and that he might disfranchise the poorer classes and keep out of the assembly men of influence who opposed him, he obtained in 1670 a law limiting the suffrage, and summoned but half the deputies elected in order to save the counties, as he claimed, half the expense of their members. Furthermore, we know that at one time he wished to set up a mint in Maryland for the coinage of money, an act of the highest sovereignty, the performance of which belonged only to the king; but he never carried out this purpose, as it was extremely doubtful if he had the right to do so under the charter. However, immediately after the restoration of his propriety in 1657, and in order to add to the dignity of his prerogative, he caused a number of coins to be struck off in England for use in the colony. These coins may have had a limited circulation, though they all had disappeared before the year 1700, but they stand as symbolic of the proprietary sovereignty that Baltimore assumed to himself.

The proprietor could not divest himself, even if he had wanted to do so, of a popular assembly, for that was provided for in the charter and had been in existence since the beginning of the colony, having first been called in 1635–though only for the second assembly, that of 1638, have the records been preserved. It had not, however, as yet attained to any such measure of strength and maturity as to take on the character of a parliamentary body. Calvert instructed his son, the governor, to call such an assembly, but at the same time he denied to it full powers of lawmaking by reserving to himself the right to initiate legislation. This reservation was in accord with the practice of the day, for we must not forget that the English Parliament did not attain full legislative supremacy till 1689, and that during the seventeenth century the right of initiating and formulating bills to be passed into law was vested to no inconsiderable extent in the king and his Privy Council. Baltimore had, therefore, some precedent upon which to base his assertion that the deputies of Maryland were not equipped either by experience or by a knowledge of law to draw up the measures that were needed for the good of the province. We know that many of these early laws were very badly phrased and that, later, expert legal assistance was often needed to aid in the planning and shaping of legislation. Baltimore was willing to call an assembly, as his charter required him to do, but he would not allow that body to exercise any other function than that of assenting to and approving such bills or laws as he or his privy council should prepare. The secretary, Baltimore's appointee, was to present these measures to the assembly for its approval or disapproval, and if they were accepted, he was to place upon them the proprietary seal. According to this view of legislation taken by the proprietor – and we must not look upon it as either illegal or preposterous – a popular assembly was called to advise and consent and not to take the initiative in shaping law for the colony. When once the assembly had won the right to initiate measures as well as to pass them – and that happened very early in most of the colonies – then it would have drawn into its own hands the reins of policy and might go wherever it pleased. But the Maryland assembly, like the Parliament of England, had not secured unequivocally that important and advantageous position in the years before 1689.

Were we to continue this analysis of the proprietary prerogatives, we could demonstrate more fully, but perhaps not more convincingly, the general statement that the years from

1660 to 1689 in the history of Maryland represent the highest point reached in the development of the power of the proprietor in any of the American colonies. No other proprietary
government, anywhere or at any time, can show such a period
as this in its history. There were struggles against proprietary
rule in all the proprietary colonies, and in all of them the
struggle was more or less successful; but nowhere else, not
even in Pennsylvania, which remained a proprietary province
to the end, was there such a rich and colorful outcropping of
proprietary pretensions as there was in Maryland during those
years. Charles Calvert, after he became proprietor, continued
to reside in the province most of the time up to 1684, when he
was obliged to return to England. He possessed a sense of proprietary dignity unmatched anywhere among the proprietors,
greater in some respects than that possessed by his far more
distinguished father. He exercised his prerogatives at a time
when Charles II and James II were on the throne and when
conditions were favorable to the enforcement of the divine
right of proprietors as well as the divine right of kings. But
just as the revolution of 1689 in England destroyed the divine
right of kings in all its manifold phases, so the revolution of
the same year in Maryland destroyed in its even more extrava-
gant manifestations the divine right of proprietors there. It
is this fact that makes the story of these years of such extraordinary interest and significance in the history of the American colonies.

The period needs a thorough and searching examination at
the hands of some competent historian with an understanding
of the larger aspects and reaches of the subject. Writers hitherto have not appreciated the full meaning of the exciting, suggestive struggle that took place. On one side we have a personal government, almost entirely in the hands of the Calvert
family and its friends, controlling the executive, administra-

tive, and judicial departments and demanding the right to initiate legislation. These powers the proprietor claimed, not in the remotest degree by gift of the people, but as his inherent right obtained through the king from God. Anticipating opposition to his rule by prerogative, Charles Calvert endeavored by proclamations, of which there are many, by acts of council, and by judgments of the courts to prevent and suppress all manner of riotous, seditious, and rebellious assemblies and meetings. As far back as 1650 his father had demanded and obtained from the assembly an act imposing upon every inhabitant of the province an ironclad oath of fidelity to himself. Later he obtained another punishing all mutinous and seditious speeches, acts, or attempts by imprisonment during his pleasure, fine, banishment, boring of the tongue, slitting of the nose, cutting off of one or both ears, whipping, or branding on the hands or forehead. Did any one deny his title to the province or dominion of Maryland or refuse to declare that he was the only true and absolute lord and proprietor to whose powers, jurisdiction, and authority all people were to submit and they and their heirs to maintain with the last drop of their blood, he was liable to the loss of hand, to death, to confiscation of all goods, to life imprisonment, or to banishment. Such a policy was not one of compromise or concession, but of coercion; it reflected the effort of a sacrosanct authority to retain its position against all comers, including the people at large in the colony.

On the other side we have this same people, against whom the chances were heavily weighted to their disadvantage. Maryland was a poor province, thinly populated in the seventeenth century, when the possession of a £10 family estate was wealth and when prosperity based on agriculture was constantly endangered not only by heavy taxation and the low price of tobacco, but also by caterpillars, heavy droughts, bad weather, and attacks from Indians by land and pirates by sea. The center of government was at St. Marys in the extreme south; the western frontier was still within the borders of Charles County, where many of the inhabitants lived in the forests; while to the north the scattered manors and plantations, ending in the extreme north with the distant estate of Augustine Hermann, lay near the water, along the banks of the Patuxent and on both shores of Chesapeake Bay. From the beginning of the colony's history, the proprietors had faced opposition to their claims and rule, and the troubles with Claiborne, Cornwallis, and Ingle, culminating in the loss by Cecilius Calvert of his control of government at the hands of the Puritans, already referred to, is a well-known incident in Maryland's story. A more serious matter was the revolt of Captain Josias Fendall, who in 1657, in imitation of parliamentary rule under the Puritan minority in England, endeavored to establish the supremacy of the assembly in Maryland. Even after the failure of this revolt and the proclamation of a general amnesty, Fendall continued to be a thorn in the flesh to the proprietor and the storm center of further trouble. As late as 1681 he was still stirring up discontent and rebellion, charging Baltimore as a Roman Catholic with encouraging the Indians to destroy the Protestants. Bacon's rebellion in Virginia found its counterpart in the Davis and Pate plot, whatever it was; and John Coode, "rank Baconist" as Baltimore called him, Godfrey, Blakeston, and others protested against taking the oath of fidelity to the proprietor and were indefatigable in fomenting trouble for the authorities. The air was charged with rumors and counter-rumors, many of them wholly false, but intensified by news from England, where the Popish Plot of 1679, the warnings of another popish plot to come in Ireland, the Presbyterian or "sham plot," as some called it, for which Stephen College suffered death and in which every effort was made to implicate the Earl of Shaftesbury, were keeping southern England in a constant state of excitement. The time was full of hysteria, when men accepted tales at their face value and believed witnesses whom they knew to be sinfully unreliable. One is amazed to note the astonishing number of this particular brand of gentry, who both in England and America made it a part of their business to bear false witness against their neighbors, to purvey false news of what those in office were doing, and to perjure themselves on any small provocation of interest or gain.

But while we know that many of the fears aroused during these years in Maryland were baseless and irrational, and that the reports of the machinations of Jesuits and Frenchmen were largely matters of the imagination, the substantial fact remains that the discontent with the proprietary government was very real and rested on sound and tangible foundations. Among ignorant and distressed planters and farmers, who were isolated in large part from the world outside, the conviction that they were being wronged and oppressed was a tremendous force driving them to action. Proprietary arrogance, social inequality, personal and political insecurity, poverty, the burden of proprietary rents and payments, and the evils of unjust administration were all playing their parts in undermining the strength of the proprietary system.

The charges against the system and those who were its supporters were many and varied. In the first place, men were realizing that the system itself was out of date and out of accord with the changing temperament of Englishmen everywhere in relation to their rulers. It is absurd to say that the existence of "his lordship's royal jurisdiction and seignory" was illegal because it was contrary to the inherent rights of Englishmen. It was perfectly legal, and Englishmen, then as now, had no other rights than those which they had won and could keep. It is enough to say that this kind of governmental organization had outlived its usefulness in America, and there were those in Maryland, as elsewhere, who felt this and in the realization of it became restless and rebellious. In the frontier region, a proprietary method of controlling lands and administering government, however much it might continue to operate in the mother country, was out of its element and in the end was bound to lose its functioning powers and die a natural death. Much water had flowed under the bridges since 1632, and it would have been well for Lord Baltimore and his relatives and friends had they seen and profited by the signs of the times. A despotism, however benevolent, or an absolute rule, however kindly and well disposed, could not have succeeded anywhere in English America in the colonial era.

In the second place, though the proprietor was generally well-intentioned, his officials and friends were neither tactful nor wise. Baltimore was harassed by many outside embarrassments, due to his strained relations with the crown over the customs situation and with William Penn over the boundaries, and at critical junctures he was obliged to absent himself from the province. Conditions did not improve at such times. The proprietary officials and members of the council were charged by their enemies in Maryland with carrying themselves "proudly and maliciously in their offices"; with possessing a turbulent spirit which "sought the utter ruin of the poor man"; with behaving "high and arrogantly" towards the people whenever the latter sought redress of their grievances; with exhibiting "huff and hector" towards those who came demanding justice; with having no mercy for the poor debtor and exacting the uttermost farthing; and with imposing fines and forfeitures that were more than the value of a planter's entire estate. Individuals protested against the imprisonment and banishment of Fendall, the arrests of Marshall, Godfrey, and others for mutinous and seditious speeches, and the hounding of any one who dared to protest against the proprietary system or the way justice was administered and the government carried on. One Abbott was convicted of heinous and abusive words against the proprietor and the lord chancellor; a Captain Wheeler was charged with uttering reviling and reproachful speeches to the derogation of the government and tending to the disturbance of the province; others for similar offenses were laid in irons, hailed before the provincial court, fined, imprisoned, and even condemned to death, though the death sentence was never executed. One, Robert Carvil of St. Marys, a man of some importance and of excellent family and an attorney in the provincial court, is reported to have said that "he was as good a Mann as my Lord, what are the Calverts? My family is as ancient as the Calverts," and his brother Thomas is reported to have added that "his Lordship was not fitt to govern the people of this Province, and that the Tower of London was a more fitt place for him than the place where he was, and that his Lordship was an old papist Rogue." Thomas's wife also came into the picture, with her complaint to Lady Baltimore at Notley Hall and her characterization of her ladyship, from whom she was unsuccessful in obtaining redress, as "the old Spiteful Toad." There can be no doubt that the discontent was widespread and by no means confined to those whose utterances are handed down in the records of the time. The revolt was not at all unlike, in spirit though not in form, other revolts in other colonies against proprietary rule – in Pennsylvania, the Jerseys, the Carolinas, and the Bahamas.

On top of all this dissatisfaction, when resistance to the prerogative and government of the Baltimores was becoming a matter of grave concern and consequence, came the fatuous conduct of those whom Baltimore entrusted with the government during his absence in England after 1684. Among these was one William Joseph, whom he finally sent over when he found he could not come himself. Joseph was sworn in as president of the council, October 3, 1688, and became acting governor of the colony. At the first meeting of the assembly he took occasion to deliver an address on the prerogative, in the manner of a sermon, which is as extraordinary as anything in colonial literature. No Stuart adherent in England or believer in the divine right of proprietors anywhere could have stated the case with more servile regard for the divinity that doth hedge in a ruler than did this obsequious official. He begged the members of the assembly, who for twenty years had been recounting in no uncertain terms their many grievances and had been as regularly told not to meddle with what did not concern them, to renew their oaths of fidelity, to stand firm in their loyalty to the existing government, and to resist to the uttermost the Machiavellian designs of those who would oppose the proprietor's beneficent rule.

Joseph's address was the last official expression of the divine right of proprietors, and the worst. Before its echoes had died away news came of the revolution in England, and the malcontents rose against the government and with almost no resistance overthrew the entire flimsy structure. The proprietary system fell, never to recover its lost position or its prestige. The new sovereigns in England, William and Mary, reserving to Baltimore his revenue, profits, and land titles unimpaired, took over the government from the victorious insurgents and in 1692 sent over Lionel Copley as the first royal governor, with instructions to organize Maryland as a royal province. This was the constitutional status of Maryland for over twenty years. The seat of government was removed from St. Marys to Annapolis, and in that removal we have more than a mere change in geographical location. St. Marys was the heart and center of the old system, the seat of the proprietary prerogative with its medieval atmosphere, the abode of the Roman Catholic influence, and the dwelling place of a form of social exclusiveness and political preferment that was fast passing away. After more than twenty years of royal control there could be no thought of returning to the conditions that had existed before 1689. Though a new proprietor was to come into possession of his inheritance in 1715 as the "absolute lord" of the province, he never again seriously tried to interfere with the onward march of the colony towards popular self-rule. The transfer of the capital was more than a matter of territorial convenience; it marked a permanent shift in the religious, political, and social center of gravity. The atmosphere changed; the feudal characteristics of proprietary government disappeared; and in Maryland, as in England at the same time, there came about a turn of events which transformed a mere survival of medievalism into something eventually modern. By 1695 the assembly and the colony itself had become predominantly Protestant, and the former was taking on, slowly, it is true, but steadily, the powers that the old proprietors had denied them — the powers of a miniature parliament, in which procedure and privilege were to become in time the outstanding features of a self-conscious and self-reliant body. Governor, council, and deputies worked together as more or less equal partners in the business of legislation, and though there was to be in the years to come a good deal of friction, particularly in money matters and in regard to Maryland's coöperation in the wars against the French and the Indians, on the whole the administration of the colony tended more and more to conform to the normal royal type. Though in name it was a proprietary colony from 1715 to 1776, the peculiarly proprietary features of the government, which had been so prominent from 1660 to 1689, were permanently thrown into the discard.

But if Maryland had succeeded in ridding herself of the worst features of proprietary government, she never, during the colonial period, freed herself from the proprietor's control of the soil of the colony. The territory of Maryland was the property of the Baltimore family, in free and common socage, for which they returned to the king an annual payment of two Indian arrows. As long as these tokens were presented, as they regularly were, the king did not interfere with Baltimore's complete possession of his landed domain. As long as he remained proprietor of the colony, he retained his title to the soil and derived therefrom a very substantial revenue, with which the assembly of the colony never meddled, though at times it opposed some of the proprietary demands. These very real and valuable profits were derived from a great variety of sources, all familiar to the English landowner, some of which brought in a good deal of money, others little or none at all. This is no place to talk at length about the proprietary system of letting out lands or of the revenues and rents arising therefrom; but I can assure you that the income from these lands and other sources were a very ready help to the members of a family that was none too well off otherwise and who looked to its estates in America as a highly profitable source of the means wherewith to live, love, and travel. These rights in Maryland, as elsewhere in the colonies, were a highly prized investment wherever proprietors were able to retain their grants of the soil from the crown, and they were fought for and defended whenever they seemed to be endangered by encroachment from any direction. It has been estimated that the Baltimore family received not less than three fifths as much as the entire cost of running the colony in the eighteenth century. The quitrents alone brought in to the Baltimore exchequer at least £8,000 a year, and if we add to these Baltimore's share of the export duty on tobacco and the profits of escheats, aliena-

tion fines, fairs, deodands, fugitives, goods of felons and sui-
cides, waifs, strays, treasure-trove and the like we can easily
raise this amount to something like £10,000 a year, a sum that
would probably mean in present values the equivalent of
$250,000. This is quite a tidy sum for Maryland to have paid
annually for the privilege of having a proprietor in her history,
proprietary names for her towns and counties, and the proprietary seal and colors for her insignia. No other English colony
in America can show such a record as this, and it stamps Maryland as the most singular and striking proprietary province in
the English portion of the New World.

We may not wonder that, in the history of the proprietary
family itself, this landed possession became the subject of a
great deal of testamentary settlement and conveyancing whenever a proprietor married and made a will in order to provide
for his widow in case of death. Several times was the province
devised to trustees to hold for wife, son, or sons; and in 1770
Frederick, Lord Baltimore, the last and least worthy of the
barons in the line of descent, bequeathed the entire family
estates to his illegitimate son, Henry Harford, and his illegitimate daughter, Frances Mary Harford, for he had no legitimate children. In 1770 Harford, a minor acting under four
guardians and executors of the will, "entered upon and took
possession of the province [as the act of confirmation reads]
and took to his use the revenues accruing from it, and did assume and exercise the sovereignty over it, as performed by
his predecessors, the former proprietors of the province, until
such time as he and his guardians were dispossessed by the
usurping powers now [1781] ruling there." As a recompense
for the proprietor's losses the State later paid Harford the
sum of $50,000.

Thus ended, fully and finally, the proprietorship of Maryland, and thus disappeared the last vestige of an outside own-

ership and authority, legally established nearly one hundred and fifty years before. It was not a glorious ending of a proprietary rule which had begun so finely with those two staunch and able men, George and Cecilius Calvert, whom Maryland so delights to honor. That the last proprietor should have been of so insignificant a character, the illegitimate son of one of the least reputable of the long line of the Calvert house, is a melancholy witness to the degeneracy that has accompanied, far too often, the later history of the English nobility.

But while thus the proprietary line was sinking into obscurity, the colony of Maryland was rising to a position of independence and strength, won after a slow and gradual exercise of the powers of self-reliance and self-government, by testing out for itself and in its own way those experiments in new ideas and practices which were to become the foundations of our political and constitutional order. Maryland's success is the more remarkable when we remember that her assembly began in a fashion unlike the beginning of any other similar colonial body, as a mixed primary and representative gathering, aristocratic in its personnel and dominated by the proprietary element. Yet despite this fact, or it may be because of it, the Maryland assembly developed a self-consciousness and sense of its own importance that in the eighteenth century made it extraordinarily and even obstinately tenacious of its constitutional rights and functions. It defied the proprietary; exercised judicial authority, even over the ordinary courts of the province; assumed parliamentary privileges almost from the day of its first recorded meeting in January 1638; enforced its rules and regulations against its own members as well as outsiders who offended its dignity – not excepting the proprietor's governor himself whenever he attempted to menace, deter, or overawe the members or interfere with the freedom of debate; and defended "the liberties of the freemen of the province." In all these things it is not surpassed by any other assembly in the history of the colonies. Others were more noisy in their conflict with royal or proprietary authority, but none was more determined, sometimes even to the injury of the province itself, to secure and retain the full powers of a parliamentary body. No other assembly, unless it be that of Virginia, followed so closely, in its practice, procedure, and legal precedents, the example of the House of Commons in England. Here, in part at least, lay the source of its strength; but even more, perhaps, was its endurance tested and its resolution sustained by the long struggle which it had been forced to carry on, for nearly a century and a half, with a feudal prerogative that had been lawfully dominant in the affairs of the colony from the beginning of its career.

We have now passed in review the many diversities of settlement which appear at the beginning of the seventeenth century. The three leading forms, viewed in the light of their origins — the commercial, the religious, and the proprietary — were all present at this early date and in their various traits and peculiarities were destined to shape and direct in very large part the later development of the colonies down even to the Revolution and after. While other influences entered in to complicate and diversify the course of events — for factors of a legal, geographic, and economic nature were to play enormously important parts in the evolution of colonial life — nevertheless, the peculiarities of early settlement were a powerful determinant as far as the spirit and bent of each individual group of colonists was concerned. The main currents of colonial progress are not to be found in the biographies of great or even of little men or in the products of literary effort and activity. They are to be found only in the daily and yearly round of actual colonial experience, in the working out of the problems which confronted the colonists in their various communities, and in the conflict of old ideas and practices, representing the inherited features and habits of a past generation, with the later needs and notions arising from contacts with new conditions in a new environment. The meaning and significance of colonial history are to be discovered not by studying selected phases of the subject, the lives of individual colonial leaders, or the mental outlook of those possessed of creative and productive literary ability, but by an understanding acquired of all phases, all men, and all constructive thought, no matter how simple and unpretentious it may be, that disclose the growth of the human colonial mind. Only thus can we hope to fathom the depths of colonial conduct and to penetrate the mysteries of colonial action, and only thus can we expect to comprehend the great issues that were at stake in this long and notable period of our national history.

INDEX

INDEX